The Apocalypse: Controversies and Meaning in Western History

Craig R. Koester, Ph.D.

THE
GREAT
COURSES®

PUBLISHED BY:

THE GREAT COURSES
Corporate Headquarters
4840 Westfields Boulevard, Suite 500
Chantilly, Virginia 20151-2299
Phone: 1-800-832-2412
Fax: 703-378-3819
www.thegreatcourses.com

Craig R. Koester, Ph.D.

Asher O. and Carrie Nasby
Professor of New Testament
Luther Seminary

Professor Craig R. Koester is the Asher O. and Carrie Nasby Professor of New Testament at Luther Seminary. He received his B.A. in 1976 from St. Olaf College and his M.Div. in 1980 from Luther Theological Seminary. He received his Ph.D. in 1986 from Union Theological Seminary and since that time has taught at Luther Seminary, where he is recognized for outstanding teaching and scholarship. In 2003, he was named an Associate of the Department of New Testament Studies at the University of Pretoria in South Africa. He also has been a guest lecturer at the Lutheran School of Theology in Oslo, Norway; at the Faculty of Theology at Comenius University in Bratislava, Slovakia; and at the Graduate Theological Union in Berkeley, California.

Professor Koester brings together the best in academic research with an engaging style of presentation. He is known for interweaving the study of biblical texts with their impact on art, literature, and music. A frequent presenter at conferences in the United States and Europe, he has also appeared in series for popular audiences, such as *The Life of Apostle Paul* with travel writer Rick Steves. He was interviewed on the book of Revelation on South African national television and has made professional translations of the book of Revelation for the Common English Bible.

A prolific scholar, Professor Koester has written the popular work *Revelation and the End of All Things* (2001) and is completing a major commentary on Revelation for Yale University Press. Among his other writings are the landmark *Hebrews: A New Translation with Introduction and Commentary* (2001), *Symbolism in the Fourth Gospel: Meaning, Mystery, Community* (2nd edition, 2003), and *Word of Life: A Theology of John's Gospel* (2008), along with numerous articles and essays. He has been a scholar in residence at the Center of Theological Inquiry and takes an active part` in the Society of

Biblical Literature, the Society for New Testament Studies, and The Catholic Biblical Association of America. He has served as associate editor for two premier journals, *New Testament Studies* and *Catholic Biblical Quarterly*.

Professor Koester has been recognized in *Who's Who in Religion* as well as *Who's Who in Biblical Studies and Archaeology*. He has received multiple grants for faculty and media development for projects such as *Bible Tutor* (http://www.bibletutor.com/), an interactive online resource that was noted in the *Los Angeles Times*.

Professor Koester lives in St. Paul, Minnesota, with his wife, Nancy. ■

Table of Contents

Table of Contents

Table of Contents

SUPPLEMENTAL MATERIAL

The Apocalypse:
Controversies and Meaning in Western History

Scope:

The Apocalypse or book of Revelation is one of the most engaging and disputed books in the Bible. It has inspired great works of art and music, and it has also fed social upheaval and speculation about the coming end of the world. This course will ask what the Apocalypse is, why it has played such a volatile role in Western culture, and how it continues to be meaningful to contemporary readers.

The first part of the course places the Apocalypse in context by exploring the intellectual and social currents that lie behind it. The lectures ask how the Hebrew prophets addressed issues of evil and hope and trace changing perspectives in Jewish apocalyptic writings, including the Dead Sea Scrolls. There is attention to the disputed question of Jesus's relationship to the apocalyptic tradition, as well as the impact of apocalyptic thought on the New Testament gospels, the letters of Paul, and the spread of early Christianity.

The second part of the course provides an overview of the Apocalypse as a literary work. We ask about the context in which the book was composed, then turn to the images that have fascinated and bewildered readers. We will ask what such images as the four horsemen, the red dragon, and the seven-headed beast might mean. As we follow the plot, with its vivid sense of struggle among God and evil and outcome in a world made new, we can see more clearly that this book offers a compelling vision of hope.

The third part of the course traces the impact that Revelation has had on Western history. Topics include disputes about the Antichrist idea and whether time would culminate in a 1,000-year period of peace on earth. We explore the reasons that Revelation was included in the New Testament when other apocalypses were not. We trace the emergence of spiritual readings of Revelation that were popular in the medieval world and the way the book was later used in conflicts among popes, emperors, and church reformers.

We will ask why some religious groups have used the Apocalypse to set dates for the end of the world, while others have seen the book as a call for a better society. Along the way, we will see how Revelation found its way into music from Bach and Handel to Dixieland jazz. In the end, we turn to the modern renaissance of interest in apocalyptic literature and its significance for readers today. ■

Revelation and the Apocalyptic Tradition
Lecture 1

The book of Revelation is one of the most intriguing and most discussed books of all time. Its pages contain a remarkable cast of characters, from a monstrous red dragon and a seven-headed beast to countless hosts of angels. It offers us terrifying scenes of cosmic conflict and glimpses of heavenly splendor. In this series of lectures, we'll investigate the background of Revelation, the text itself, and the impact it has had on Western culture. Along the way, we'll ask: What draws people to the Apocalypse? How was the book read in its own time? And what does it have to say about spiritual life in the present?

Famous Students of the Apocalypse

- Sir Isaac Newton, one of the most famous scientists of all time, was fascinated by Revelation. Newton believed that he could decipher the mysteries of Revelation in much the same way that he could decipher the mysteries of the natural world: by formulating laws for the interpretation of apocalyptic writings.

- Newton thought that Revelation could be used as a telescope, to peer not into the mysteries of space but the mysteries of time and history. He further believed that these mysteries were unfolding with mathematical precision. According to Newton, Revelation had accurately predicted the rise of Constantine, the tribal invasions of the Roman Empire, and the fall of the city of Constantinople.

- Another famous figure who was fascinated with Revelation was the British novelist D. H. Lawrence. Near the end of his life, Lawrence wrote a book called *Apocalypse*, in which he called Revelation unpoetic, ugly, and vindictive. He insisted that its violent imagery was the opposite of the message of love that Jesus brought.

Outline of the Course

- This course is designed in three parts. The first part considers the background of the Apocalypse; the second looks at the contents of the book itself; and the third part explores what happened after the book was written, as people have tried to make sense of it over the centuries.

- An important piece of the background concerns the word "apocalypse" itself. Today, the word conjures images of disaster and destruction, but the author of Revelation used it to mean "disclosure"; that is, an apocalypse is an act of

Often depicted as a cataclysmic event as seen here, the Apocalypse can also invoke images of God's throne in a heavenly city adorned with pearly gates and golden streets.

disclosure. The original Greek word *apokálypsis*, the first word in the book, is translated into English as "revelation" to convey the sense of giving insight into mystery.

The Two Mysteries of Apocalyptic Writings

- Apocalyptic writings often revolve around two basic mysteries that have concerned people across time, geography, and religious tradition: the nature of evil and the nature of hope.

- The book of Revelation draws some perspectives on evil and hope from the tradition of the Hebrew prophets, such figures as Isaiah, Jeremiah, and Ezekiel. These prophets weren't concerned with predicting the future so much as shaping life in the present. In their view, corruption, brutality, and injustice were everywhere. They open up a disturbing vision of the world and its people in the presence of God.

- In the realm of hope, the prophets are unwilling to let the world be satisfied with meager hopes and ordinary dreams. They open up vistas of peace and wonder that encompass all nations and transform Creation itself.

The Apocalyptic Tradition
- The prophetic tradition eventually gave birth to the apocalyptic tradition, an important development that also lies behind the book of Revelation. This tradition depicts the world as a place in which the forces of good and evil are in conflict and focuses on disclosing the nature of this conflict in order to give readers confidence that the just and righteous purposes of God will win out.

- The apocalyptic tradition informed some of the writers of the Dead Sea Scrolls and other ancient Jewish sources. It also had an important place in early Christianity. The New Testament gospels tell of Jesus announcing the coming reign of God, the coming kingdom of God, and the accomplishment of God's designs for the world.

- The apostle Paul attests to the power of the apocalyptic tradition in the way he describes the struggle between the power of sin and the power of grace, the power of death against the power of life.

The Book of Revelation
- The book of Revelation was written in Greek nearly 2,000 years ago. Although bits and pieces of Revelation are often taken out of context, we will read it as a piece of literature with its own integrity.

- The beginning of the book contains messages to seven churches, which were located in the Roman province of Asia Minor, in what today is the country of Turkey. These messages tell us about the book's earliest readers and the challenges they faced in the cities where they lived.

- In the middle of the book, we find scenes of struggle, in which the challenges of the readers are shown to be part of conflict on a cosmic scale.

- On one side of this conflict is the Creator of the world and the source of all life. With him is the Lamb, who brings deliverance through the power of self-sacrifice. Their work leads to the New Jerusalem, which holds the promise of life for all nations.

- On the other side are the forces of destruction, depicted as a dragon and a beast. Their base of operation is a city known as Babylon, which debases life and oppresses the nations of the world.

- The struggle reaches its climax at the end of the book, when evil is finally overcome, justice prevails, and the world itself is made new.

Word Pictures in Revelation
- The writer of Revelation used pictures, such as the dragon, the beast, and the Lamb. Some have argued that the word pictures were a form of secret code that would reveal meaning to some but hide it from others. As mentioned, however, an apocalypse was meant to be a disclosure, a book that offered people a new way of seeing.

- The Apocalypse is like other forms of art in that it gives us a different perspective on the world, one that is startling and challenging. The writer uses wild colors and fantastic images that shape the way people see the power of evil, the nature of hope, the character of God, and the character of the world.

- It's also important for us to read Revelation contextually, that is, as its first readers nearly 2,000 years ago would have understood it.

The Impact of Revelation on Western Culture
- In the third part of the course, when we look at the impact of Revelation on Western culture, we'll meet a colorful cast of characters that includes prophets and mystics, popes and emperors, theologians, journalists, composers, and slaves.

- What questions drove these people to Revelation? And why is it that people since ancient times have tried to turn Revelation into a roadmap for the end of the world? We will explore these questions later in the course.

- We will also explore what Revelation might have to say about spiritual life in the present. The book opens up a transcendent world in which the presence of God is vivid and palpable. It invites people to consider what it means to live in the presence of God and how that shapes a way of life in the world.

Suggested Reading

Heschel, *The Prophets*, vol. 1, chap. 1.

Murrin, "Newton's Apocalypse."

Questions to Consider

1. Isaac Newton regarded Revelation as a fascinating code that could be deciphered and related to world events. By way of contrast, D. H. Lawrence thought that Revelation was a harmful book that should not be taken seriously. Have you encountered more recent examples of those who either speculate about the book or dismiss it? What other perceptions of the book are you familiar with?

2. The words "prophet" and "prophecy" have a range of connotations. Some equate prophecy with predicting the future. Others think of prophetic voices more broadly for those who issue sharp critiques of modern society or offer bold visions for future action. How are these ideas of what is prophetic either similar to or different from the perspectives on Hebrew prophecy that were suggested by the lecture?

Apocalyptic Worldview in Judaism
Lecture 2

In this lecture and the next, we will explore how the apocalyptic worldview came into being and why it was so important in the ancient world. We will first look at the way the Hebrew prophets dealt with themes of evil and hope, then see how these prophetic perspectives took on new forms in Jewish apocalyptic writings. We'll also touch on one of the central concerns of early apocalyptic writings that remains valid today: Given that the world is unfair, what gives people the courage to live lives of integrity?

The World of the Ancient Prophets

- The Jewish scholar Abraham Heschel called the ancient prophets "some of the most disturbing people who have ever lived." The words of the prophets are urgent and alarming, as if communicated directly from the heart of God to man.

- These prophets were not predictors of the future, but they speak about the future in order to disclose what is at stake in the present. They give warnings and exhortations that are designed to startle people into living their lives differently and committing themselves to a different future.

- According to Heschel, basic to the prophets' worldview is an overwhelming awareness of the presence of God and their accountability to him. The author of Revelation had a similar sense of God.

- The author of Revelation and others who wrote apocalyptic texts were unwilling to leave people in a closed universe. They were driven to draw people more deeply into the mystery of God.

The Problem of Evil

- It is helpful to think about the problem of evil in prophetic writings with an image of three concentric circles. At the center, the prophets speak about the evils among the people of Israel. In the middle is a wider circle of concern with evil in other nations. Finally, the outer circle is where the prophets speak in sweeping terms about the suffering of the entire world as a result of evil.

- Beginning with the inner circle, Isaiah castigates the people of Israel for their corrupt use of power and their indifference toward the vulnerable members of society. He lashes out against those who try to cover up their wrongdoing with a façade of religiosity.

- Moving outward, the next ring of concern addresses other nations, such as the Assyrian Empire (engaged in a brutal campaign of conquest at the time of Isaiah), Babylonia, Syria, Egypt, and Ethiopia. The prophets warned that those who perpetrated violence would eventually become victims of violence, perhaps in a cataclysmic battle, in which God would ultimately defeat the hostile nations.

- The outer ring of concern takes on a cosmic dimension. The prophets warn, "The earth shall be utterly laid waste and despoiled." It "lies polluted under its inhabitants, for they have transgressed laws, violated statutes, and broken the everlasting covenant. Therefore a curse devours the earth, and its inhabitants suffer for their guilt."

The Prophets' Messages of Hope

- The prophets also offer messages of hope that can be envisaged with our image of concentric circles. At the center, Ezekiel, for example, pictures the people of Israel as a collection of dry bones, but the breath of God blows on them and fills the bones with life. Ezekiel also gives us a vision of the renewal of the city of Jerusalem, filled by the Lord with a dazzling radiance.

- The second chapter of Isaiah offers a vision of hope that may be familiar to anyone who has seen the monument at U.N. Headquarters in New York City. Isaiah says that all the nations "shall beat their swords into plowshares and their spears into pruning hooks. Nation shall not lift up sword against nation. Neither shall they learn war anymore."

© Photos.com/Getty Images/Thinkstock.

Ezekiel's vision of God's heavenly throne in a crystal dome is similar to the one later described by the author of the book of Revelation.

- Finally, the prophets hope for the transformation of the earth as a whole and the ability to overcome death. A passage in Isaiah states that the Lord God "will swallow up death forever," which will mean the elimination of grief. At the end of Isaiah, we are treated to a vision of a renewed earth, imbued with life and peace.

The Emergence of the Apocalyptic Tradition

- The apocalyptic tradition emerged in Jewish circles after the 5th century B.C. An apocalyptic text is one that offers insight into the mysteries of God, the world, and the human situation.

- The apocalyptic tradition differs from the older prophetic tradition in its theme of dualism. We often see in apocalyptic writings a sharp contrast between the powers of good and evil. There is a contrast, too, between the present age, in which evil is operative, and the coming age, when only goodness will prevail.

- This dualism is readily apparent in some of the Dead Sea Scrolls, a collection of Jewish texts written a little more than 2,000 years ago and hidden in caves near the Dead Sea sometime in the mid-1st century.

- One of these texts is called the Rule of the Community, or the Manual of Discipline. Its author tells us that God alone is supreme, but two forces are at work in the world under God's authority: the spirit of truth and the spirit of deceit. With the two spirits are two angelic powers: the Prince of Light and the Angel of Darkness. The effects of these conflicting powers are seen in the behaviors they generate in human beings.

- The writer of this scroll sees people involved in a struggle of cosmic proportions, a vision that goes a step beyond the prophetic tradition. The prophets spoke of good and evil largely in human terms, but the writer of the Dead Sea text sees evil as a demonic force that is operative in the world and tries to bring people under its influence.

- Another hallmark of the apocalyptic tradition is the sense that the struggle between good and evil will continue throughout the present age. Human nature was not expected to improve, but God would ultimately bring about a decisive change in current conditions, inaugurating a new era.

- The sharp temporal distinction between the present and the future in the Jewish apocalyptic tradition is seen in the Dead Sea text known as the War of the Sons of Light and the Sons of Darkness. In this scroll, the older prophetic theme of God's final battle against hostile nations is elevated to a cosmic scale.

The Apocalyptic Text of Daniel

- Daniel is the one Jewish apocalyptic text that made its way into the Hebrew Bible (the Christian Old Testament). The text is an apocalypse in the technical sense of a narrative that discloses things about the heavenly realm of God and the course of life on earth.

- The apocalyptic visions in the last half of Daniel trace the flow of history, showing us the rise and fall of empires through fantastic and bizarre word pictures.

- The author of Daniel traces the relentless succession of empires down to his own time in the 2nd century B.C. At that time, a ruler from Syria named Antiochus Epiphanes suppressed Jewish religious practices and turned the Jerusalem Temple into the sanctuary of a foreign god.

- For Daniel, it made no sense that those who tried to follow traditional Jewish ways should suffer this "desolating sacrilege." A just God should reward the righteous and punish the wicked, but that had not happened.

- According to Daniel, though, it would happen. Daniel shows that one after another, all forms of tyranny will fall. Conflict may escalate at the end of the age, but finally, this pattern will be brought to an end so that God's justice can be carried out. The focus of hope is on the coming kingdom of God.

- A central player in this drama is a figure known as the Son of Man, who will be given everlasting dominion over all peoples, nations, and languages. Of course, later, this messianic figure was identified as the risen Jesus.

- According to Daniel, the current age would end with a resurrection of the dead and a time of judgment. The promise of resurrection develops the prophetic hope for God's coming victory over death. The resurrection is also connected with God's justice; Daniel envisions it as the time when people will be held accountable to God.

- Life was often unjust for the original readers of Daniel. In their experience, those who followed the ways of God suffered for their beliefs. For these readers to remain true to their convictions, they needed a sense that justice would win out.

- Although modern readers of Daniel generally live in less threatening circumstances, a similar question remains valid: If the world is unfair, what gives people the courage to live lives of integrity? Daniel insisted that people could remain committed to what was just because God's purposes would eventually be fulfilled.

Suggested Reading

Collins, *The Apocalyptic Imagination*.

Nickelsburg, *Jewish Literature between the Bible and the Mishnah*.

Questions to Consider

1. Some apocalyptic writings understand evil to be a cosmic power that works in the world. Some identify the principal agent of evil as a supernatural being, such as Belial or Satan. Why might early readers of apocalyptic literature have found it helpful to think of evil as a cosmic power? What problems might arise from this worldview?

2. Some apocalyptic writings expect there to be a resurrection of the dead and final judgment at the end of the age. How might such a vision of the future have affected the way readers thought of life in the present?

Apocalyptic Dimension of Early Christianity
Lecture 3

I n this lecture, we move into the world of early Christianity, which emerged from the rich matrix of ancient Judaism. Indeed, Jesus's relationship to the different traditions of Judaism, combined with his own complex character, complicate our task of examining how the apocalyptic worldview was taken up and transformed by early Christian writers in the New Testament. In this lecture, we'll look at how the legacy of Jesus redefined classic Jewish apocalyptic thought and placed Christians at a juncture between the present age and the age to come.

The Shift of Apocalypticism in Early Christianity

- The classic paradigm for Jewish apocalyptic thought consisted of two ages: the present age, in which the powers of sin, evil, and death are at work, and the age to come, in which there will be only life and righteousness.

- The classic scenario expects God to act in a definitive way to end the present age by defeating the powers of evil. The new age will begin with the resurrection of the dead. In this scenario, there is a direct movement from one age into the next.

- For early Christians, the legacy of Jesus redefined this paradigm. It was no longer a straightforward movement from the present age into the new age. Instead, the new age began before the old age was fully gone, and Christians found themselves at the juncture of the two.

- As they looked to the past, early Christians believed that the world had been changed by the coming of Jesus. In their eyes, his life, death, and resurrection had been God's way of intervening in the world. The result was that things were no longer the same.

- Yet when they looked at the present, these Christians realized that the powers of sin and death were still operative. Jesus had risen from the dead, but others had not. For these Christians, the resurrection remained a future hope.

- Early Christians lived between these two realities: the resurrection of Jesus, which had already happened, and the resurrection of others, which was yet to occur.

The Gospel of Mark
- These peculiar apocalyptic dynamics helped to shape the Gospel of Mark. In the opening chapter of Mark, Jesus declares, "the kingdom of God has come near."

- Mark makes it clear that the coming of the kingdom means that God will deal with the forces of evil that oppose him and oppress his people. Jesus's call for repentance in Mark is a call for the realignment of loyalties, away from sin and toward the ways of God.

- At many points in Mark's gospel, the kingdom of God seems to be already present, a power already at work in the world through Jesus. Still, throughout the gospel, there is a relentless sense of movement into the future.

- The conclusion of Mark's story, which brings together Jesus's teachings about the end of the age and the story of his crucifixion, both preserves and decisively alters the traditional apocalyptic paradigm. The turning of the ages becomes connected to the crucifixion and resurrection of Jesus.

- Jesus's teachings about the end of the age are found most dramatically in Mark 13. Here, Jesus initially lays out a traditional apocalyptic scenario that draws heavily on Daniel and the Hebrew prophets. As we read further, however, we find that the apocalyptic struggle has already begun in the story of Jesus himself.

- The apocalyptic hope of resurrection begins to be realized with the news that Jesus has risen from the dead. In Mark's gospel, the new age has come in Jesus before the old age has fully ended.

Jesus's Impact on the Apocalyptic Paradigm

- Jesus's impact on the apocalyptic paradigm had major ramifications for the way his followers understood God, themselves, and their futures.

- First, with Jesus, the nature of God's kingdom is redefined. During his ministry, Jesus had linked the kingdom to love for God and for others; thus, proclaiming Jesus as king at the time of his crucifixion discloses the lengths to which love will go. If the cross is an apocalyptic action through which God confronts the forces of evil, then it is an action that takes the form of complete self-giving.

- Second, Jesus defines the direction of the action as one that goes through death into life. Suffering is not an end in itself; it is the path that love and service take in the kingdom of God.

- Finally, the belief that Jesus had risen from the dead meant that he fit the role of the Son of Man pictured in Daniel. He was the one whose coming in glory would complete the turning of the ages by gathering people into his kingdom through the resurrection of the dead.

For many Christian writers, as well as the writer of Revelation, the crucifixion and resurrection were essential parts of the Christian story.

The Gospel of Matthew

- This altered apocalyptic paradigm informed people's perspectives in different ways. We can see these changes in the Gospel of Matthew, written some years later than Mark.

- In some places, Matthew heightens the sense of the apocalyptic change that has already occurred by speaking about the earth itself shaking at the time of Jesus's crucifixion and his resurrection. Matthew also gives a more expansive picture of the end of the age that is yet to come, offering a description of the last judgment by the Son of Man.

- Matthew pictures the present, which falls between the First and Second Coming of Christ, as a time when things are mixed. The good news of the kingdom has already been planted, yet the evil one continues to contaminate the crop with weeds.

The Acts of the Apostles

- The Acts of the Apostles, written by Luke, tells the story of the early church, from the time of Jesus's resurrection through the work of his followers over the next several decades.

- If the hope was that the Son of Man would gather in the faithful at the end of the age, then the book of Acts shows Jesus sending the Spirit to empower the disciples to create a community of faith in the here and now.

The Gospel of John

- The Gospel of John moves even further in seeing the promise of the future as a reality in the present. A good example of this is the change in the apocalyptic theme of resurrection.

- The Gospel of John recognizes that life and death have physical dimensions, yet John also assumes that life has a relational dimension. People were created for relationships with God and with other people, and when those relationships are damaged, people are not fully alive.

- According to John's gospel, the coming of Jesus is the apocalyptic event that transforms the promise of resurrection into a present reality. John identifies love as the center of Jesus's legacy and says that Jesus came in order to convey the fullness of divine love to the world. Jesus's willingness to die was the most radical form of divine love.

- When the reality of divine love evokes a response of faith in human beings, their relationship with God is restored. And from John's perspective, that restoration of relationship is where eternal life begins.

The Apostle Paul

- The apocalyptic tension between the present and the future profoundly shaped the work of Paul in the letters he wrote to Christian congregations. At some points in his letters, Paul looks back and insists that the new age truly began in Jesus. Elsewhere, he looks ahead and says that neither he nor his readers has fully arrived in the kingdom of God.

- A good example of Paul's emphasis on the apocalyptic change that has already taken place is his Letter to the Galatians, addressing the question of circumcision in some Christian communities. Paul argues that in the old age, the regulations of the Jewish law had helped to keep human sin in check; now, however, God has taken on the problem of sin through the death of Jesus.

- In First Corinthians, Paul gives greater emphasis to the future. Here, Paul reminds the Corinthians that their exuberant experience of the Spirit is not ultimate. In the future, both prophecy and ecstatic speech will end, but faith, hope, and love will abide.

- For Paul, death is the great adversary. In his eyes, death is not merely what occurs with a person's last breath but the whole process of suffering and illness that culminates in the cessation of life. The apocalyptic battle that God is now waging in Christ must continue until death itself has been brought to nothing.

- The act of raising Jesus from the dead marked the onset of a new age that will culminate in the final resurrection of the dead. Through that final resurrection, Paul says that God will destroy the power of death through his sheer gift of life. That is the essence of the apocalyptic hope for Paul: a vision in which death is swallowed up in the victory that comes through life.

Suggested Reading

Allison, "The Eschatology of Jesus."

de Boer, "Paul and Apocalyptic Eschatology."

Questions to Consider

1. Some passages in the New Testament gospels say that God's kingdom "has come near" or "is among you." These emphasize the nearness of God's reign. Other passages expect the kingdom to come in the future, brought in by a time of affliction, then salvation when the faithful are gathered together. In what way do these different emphases seem contradictory? How might early Christians have considered these ideas to be compatible?

2. Paul believed that through Jesus, the powers of grace and life, which belong to the coming age, had invaded the old age of evil and death. He expected the conflict to end with the final defeat of death at Christ's Second Coming. How might this worldview encourage people to engage creatively with the world around them? Conversely, how might it encourage people to disengage from the world?

Origins of the Book of Revelation
Lecture 4

In the last two lectures, we've considered the background of Revelation. We began with the Hebrew prophets and traced the themes of evil and hope through their writings into the Jewish apocalyptic tradition. We then considered the way in which the apocalyptic worldview, with its strong sense of conflicting powers, was taken up and transformed in early Christian thought. In this lecture, we begin our study of the book of Revelation itself, exploring its origins and the character of its author, John.

How Did Revelation Originate?
- The book of Revelation offers only a few tantalizing details about the circumstances in which it was written. According to the first chapter, it was composed by someone named John, who received visions on the island of Patmos in the Aegean Sea.

- Legends arose that the author of the book was actually the apostle John. To this day on the island of Patmos, visitors can see the Cave of the Apocalypse, where John is supposed to have received his revelation from God.

- Historians today generally grant that the author's name was, in fact, John. This observation sets Revelation apart from most other apocalypses, whose authors often adopted pen names.

- Despite the legends, most modern historians do not believe that the author of Revelation was the apostle John, at least in part because he never claims to be an apostle and the only encounter he describes with Christ is his vision.

- John calls himself simply a "servant" of Christ and a "brother" of the Christians to whom he is writing. He was likely a Jewish Christian who lived and worked in the Roman province of Asia during the last decades of the 1st century.

© Photos.com/Getty Images/Thinkstock.

The island of Patmos is where John, the composer of the book of Revelation, received his visions. Despite legends to the contrary, he was unlikely one of Christ's apostles.

The Character of John

- John begins the book of Revelation using the common form of an ancient letter. He addresses his letter to "the seven churches that are in Asia" and sends a greeting of grace and peace in the name of God.

- John's use of the Greek language, however, is the most peculiar in the entire New Testament. For example, the modern translation of his greeting is usually something like this: "Grace to you and peace from the one who is, and who was, and who is to come. The Almighty." In contrast, a literal translation would read: "Grace to you and peace, from He the Is, and from He the Was, and from He the Coming One."

- Why is John's grammar so convoluted? One explanation is that his native language may have been Hebrew and he spoke Greek as a second language. However, some scholars have pointed out that in other parts of Revelation, John's grammar flows effortlessly. He may have chosen to break the rules of grammar to make a point.

- John's usage is comparable to that of a teenager who chooses not to speak proper English because it is associated with people in authority. The language is deliberately nonconformist and defiant. Because John's message was countercultural—outside the mainstream of Greek and Roman society—he may have chosen to convey it in a countercultural form of speech. There is a quality in his writing that defies social convention.

- John's lack of conformity and subversive message were apparently dangerous enough to authorities that he was banished to the island of Patmos. From John's perspective, he was sent to Patmos because of his religions convictions, but the Romans, generally tolerant of a variety of religious traditions, must have discerned something more troubling in John's message.

- As we read further in the book, we'll find that there was indeed much in what John was saying that would make the Romans uneasy. He was highly critical of the status quo and sharp in his criticism of Roman social and economic practices—a strong advocate for change.

- According to Roman law, the appropriate punishment for "superstition" (any religious belief that the Romans found suspect) was banishment to one of various islands in the Aegean Sea. In the time of John, the island of Patmos was quite ordinary, prompting us to wonder why anyone would have listened to its one troubling resident, John.

John's Role as a Prophet

- Prophets played an important role in some Christian communities of the late 1st century. These prophets understood themselves to share in the wider tradition of Hebrew prophecy, which was known to them through Scripture.

- In a previous lecture, we noted that such prophets as Isaiah and Ezekiel conveyed a vivid sense of standing in the presence of God. Some of these prophets recounted their experiences of God, recalling what it was like to sense his overwhelming majesty and to feel compelled by God to speak words of judgment and hope to the people.

- John locates himself in this tradition of earlier prophets when he recounts his own spiritual experience in the first chapter of his book. He describes seeing the majestic figure of Jesus, whose face was as radiant as the sun. Around Jesus were seven golden lampstands, symbolizing the seven churches to which the readers belonged. When John experienced this vision, he was overwhelmed and fell to the ground.

- Some modern interpreters note that John's description of his awe-inspiring encounter with Christ follows a typical literary form; ancient writers of apocalypses often described a similar sense of being in the divine presence. Other scholars believe that there could be a genuine spiritual experience behind the early passages of Revelation.

- It's important to note that people in antiquity generally agreed that spiritual experiences did occur, but they also understood that such experiences did not guarantee the legitimacy of the prophet. In First Corinthians, Paul expects the members of the congregation to weigh the messages shared by those who feel moved by the Spirit to speak. Not everything a prophet said was to be taken as a direct message from heaven.

- In Revelation, John himself mentions a group of prophets whose work he valued, but he also refers to a woman at Thyatira whose prophecy he disputed. For early Christians, what mattered most was whether a prophet's message was congruent with what they knew of God.

"An Apocalypse from Jesus Christ"

- The first line in John's writing tells his readers what to expect: an apocalypse, that is, a disclosure, a way of seeing. For John, this disclosure will address God, the world, and the readers themselves, because these things are all interrelated. In an apocalyptic worldview, none of them can be adequately considered apart from the others.

- John also tells his readers that his disclosure will show them "what must soon take place." That line has sent many people into the realm of speculation; the assumption is that John is promising to tell them how soon the end of the world will take place, yet John makes no such promise.

- In chapters 2 and 3, we learn that John's focus is not on the end of the world but on life in this world, where his readers are experiencing various challenges.

- In the coming chapters, John will tell his readers what must take place in the context of their lives: The struggling are to persevere; the complacent are to become recommitted; and those in the middle are called to a renewed sense of integrity in a complicated world.

Suggested Reading

Collins, *Crisis and Catharsis*.

Schüssler Fiorenza, "Apokalypsis and Propheteia."

Questions to Consider

1. Interpreters have debated whether the writer of Revelation was John the apostle, one of Jesus's original disciples. How might those who assume that the writer was one of the apostles read Revelation differently from those who think that he was a prophet living later in the 1st century? Does this issue make a difference for your reading of Revelation? Why or why not?

2. The way people picture the author's situation can affect the way they read Revelation. How might those who picture the author in a rather ordinary Greek community on Patmos read the Apocalypse differently from those who assume that he is undergoing harsh imprisonment?

Issues Facing Revelation's First Readers
Lecture 5

I n the last lecture, we got acquainted with the mysterious figure named John, the writer of the book of Revelation. In this one, we turn to a related question, which is the identity and situation of his intended readers. This question is an intriguing and important one in light of the many popular interpretations of Revelation, especially those that find in it plots to achieve global control in the 21st century. As we will learn, John was actually addressing specific communities of Christians facing certain difficulties. His purpose was not to confuse them but to challenge and encourage them. Knowing something about this ancient context may make Revelation more relevant for modern readers because it allows us to see how it spoke to real-life situations from the moment it was written.

The Ancient Readers of Revelation
- The opening chapter of Revelation tells us that the book was first addressed to the Christian communities in seven cities of the Roman province of Asia or Asia Minor. Today, this region is the western part of Turkey, along the Aegean Sea.

- Among the cities mentioned are Ephesus, a vibrant commercial center and the largest city in Asia Minor; Smyrna, the birthplace of Homer; and Pergamum, known for its temple to the goddess Athena. The other cities are Thyatira, Sardis, Philadelphia, and Laodicea, each with its own local industries, temples, and forms of civic life.

- In all of these cities, the dominant language and culture was Greek. All belonged to the Roman Empire, and all had communities of Christians. Why did these Christians need to hear John's visionary message? Because all of these congregations struggled with issues of persecution, assimilation, and complacency.

Persecution

- Revelation mentions persecution specifically in connection with the Christians at Smyrna, who were being publicly slandered or denounced by a group of opponents. John warns that these Christians might be put into prison or even killed because of their faith, but he calls on them to remain faithful in the face of hostility.

- It is easy to see why the visions of cosmic conflict later in the book would have been meaningful to these persecuted Christians. When John tells of a seven-headed beast rising out of the sea to persecute the faithful, the Christians at Smyrna would have agreed that this fit their experience.

- Many people assume that the Roman persecution of Christians began when the emperor commanded that all citizens must worship him or face the consequences. Indeed, the emperor Domitian, who was probably in power at the time Revelation was written, is said to have issued a decree insisting that everyone address him as *dominus et deus* ("lord and god"). This was appalling even from a Roman point of view.

- Some ancient historians suggested that as Domitian's megalomania grew, so did his paranoia and persecution of those he suspected of disloyalty. If this picture of the rising threat is accurate, then we might assume that John was warning his readers about something that was clear to all—an impending campaign of terror against the church, sponsored by the Roman state.

- Recent historical research, however, has shown that the threat of terror was not as readily apparent as originally thought. Roman life in the time of Domitian seems to have gone on much as it had for years, especially in places that were far from the capital in Rome. In fact, scholars have found no evidence that Domitian insisted on being addressed as lord and god.

- It's also important to note that the cult of the Roman emperors was not so much imposed from the top down as it was developed from the bottom up. It probably originated about 100 years before Revelation was written, when the people of Asia Minor requested and received permission to build a temple in honor of Augustus. Later temples were built in honor of Tiberius (in Smyrna) and Domitian (in Ephesus).

- The early chapters of Revelation indicate that persecution was local and sporadic, growing out of uneasiness about the presence of Christians in the community. These Christians, unlike the Greeks and Romans, worshiped only one God, and unlike the Jews, they put their faith in a crucified and risen messiah named Jesus. They may have respected the emperor, but they referred to Jesus as their king.

- When their fellow citizens grew uneasy about the Christians, they sometimes denounced them to the Roman authorities, who would investigate the situation. If the Christians seemed to be intractable, they could be put to death. But this kind of action tended to remain local; there was no widespread campaign to stamp out the church.

Assimilation

- Some Christians may have faced open hostility, but others had to deal with more subtle pressures to conform. How could they remain true to their convictions while interacting socially with those who did not share their faith?

- The specific question that raised the issue of assimilation was whether or not it was acceptable for Christians to eat food that had been sacrificed to one of the Greek or Roman gods. The cities of Asia Minor often had local religious festivals that were major social events. Could Christians participate in the banquets associated with these festivals without compromising their convictions?

- The issue of assimilation also came up in connection with the practice of dining at temples to the Greek and Roman gods. Social gatherings were often held at temples, and attendance brought honor to the god or goddess associated with the temple. Christians invited to such gatherings were faced with the dilemma of compromising their convictions if they accepted or alienating their friends or business associates if they refused.

- In such situations, Christians did not face violent persecution but the challenge to maintain the integrity of their beliefs while living in an interreligious world.

Complacency

- The issue of complacency is most evident in Revelation in the message to the church at Laodicea. John declares that the Christians there are tepid in their faith because of their wealth. The material comfort of these Christians has sapped away the vitality of their faith.

- The Christians at Laodicea and some other places were apparently thriving in the Roman-era economy. The Romans had built roads and enhanced the possibilities for trade and commerce on an ever-widening scale. Local markets expanded into regional and international markets, and local trade flourished. The Christians at Laodicea must have participated in the prosperous economy.

- These people were not preoccupied with the shadow of Roman persecution but with the brightness of their own economic future. According to Revelation, they were happy to practice the Christian faith as long as it did not become too intense or uncomfortable.

Messages for Ancient Readers

- It's interesting to ask whether any analogies exist between the ancient situations we have described and the experiences of modern readers. We can also explore how the message of Revelation might sound from different vantage points.

- For readers who feel threatened, Revelation can be a source of encouragement to keep the faith in the face of hostility. As the visions later unfold in scenes of cosmic conflict, they take us far beyond the kind of local persecution that some of the ancient readers experienced. The writer uses the images of the beast and the dragon to show people that their own local struggles are part of a much larger story.

- The author also recognizes that in some situations, the faithful are the ones who suffer most at the hands of their opponents. In such a world, there is little incentive to resist, but by placing the local conflict within the larger story of God and evil, Revelation gives readers a reason to persevere. They are told that the future ultimately belongs to God, not to the Roman state or any other power.

- For readers who are grappling with more subtle pressures to compromise their beliefs in order to assimilate, the visions of Revelation may act as a challenge. The compromises required to stay within the mainstream of social life in Asia Minor may have seemed innocent enough when taken on their own, but the visions of Revelation highlight the contrast between good and evil much more emphatically.

- Finally, the wealthy readers of Revelation may find its visions both disturbing and challenging. Where wealth blinded them to the reality of evil in their world, Revelation called them to open their eyes. Where prosperity made them oblivious to failings in themselves and their community, Revelation summoned them to take stock of the truth. The goal was not to make them despair but to cultivate a deeper sense of engagement on the side of God against the destroyers of the earth.

Suggested Reading

deSilva, *Seeing Things John's Way*, pp. 29–63.

Koester, *Revelation and the End of All Things*, pp. 41–69.

Questions to Consider

1. Revelation originally addressed readers who faced different kinds of challenges. On one end of the spectrum were those who faced local harassment or persecution. On the other end of the spectrum were those who were prosperous and complacent. Why might it be helpful to keep both kinds of readers in mind when reading Revelation?

2. Some early readers faced challenges related to assimilation. How far could they compromise their beliefs before they lost their integrity? In the 1st century, the disputed issue was whether the followers of Jesus could eat what had been sacrificed to Greco-Roman deities. What situations might be analogous for modern readers? When might people today have to ask how far they can compromise their convictions before they lose their integrity?

God, the Lamb, and the Seven Seals
Lecture 6

Thus far, we have considered what the first several chapters of Revelation tell us about the author and his early readers. In this lecture, we move more deeply into the Apocalypse and take up what is probably its most challenging dimension: its word pictures. We'll look in particular at the four horsemen, who bring threats of war, hardship, and death to the people of the world. But every bit as important as these disturbing images are the other scenes that John pictures, those that take readers into the realms of heaven.

The Throne Room of God

- At the beginning of chapter 4, John makes a visionary journey through the open door of heaven. There, he sees a majestic throne room, arranged in concentric circles. At the center of the vision is the throne of God.

- The next circle consists of four mysterious creatures surrounding the throne. Their faces resemble those of a lion, an ox, a human being, and an eagle. All have six wings and are covered with eyes.

- Here, John is giving us a vision of a rightly ordered universe, with the Creator at the center, surrounded by heavenly representatives of Creation. Their faces include those of wild and domesticated animals, along with human beings and birds.

- This imagery recalls depictions of God's majesty from the Hebrew prophets, but John also includes new details that might make this scene uncomfortably relevant for at least some of his readers. The next circle consists of 24 elders, their own thrones encircling that of God. "Elder" was a title for those who led Jewish and early Christian communities by their wise counsel and by the example they set.

- The elders in Revelation cast down their crowns before God, providing an example of true worship. The gesture of giving a golden crown to a figure on a throne did not come from the Hebrew prophets but from the political world of the Greeks and Romans.

- The Roman world had its own concentric circles of power. At the center was the emperor, who was surrounded by an inner circle of admirers and friends. This inner circle led the rest of society in praising the worth of both the emperor and the traditional gods. Some of John's early readers seemed to be comfortable with this arrangement and found ways to make it work for them socially and economically.

- But John's picture of the heavenly throne room presses for clarity about his readers' most fundamental commitments. Do their highest loyalties truly belong to the state, or do they have a higher loyalty to God?

The Vision of the Seven Seals
- In the next chapter of Revelation, John tells us that God holds a scroll in his hand, sealed with seven seals so that it cannot be read. An angel asks, "Who is worthy to open the scroll and break its seals?" But the reply comes back that no one in heaven or on earth is worthy.

- One of the elders then tells John that the Lion of the tribe of Judah, the Root of David, has conquered, so he can open the scroll. The lion was a traditional image for power and majesty, while the Root of David is an expression used for the heir to David's throne. Readers believe that they will meet this conquering hero, who will open the scroll and carry out the will of God.

- Instead of a Lion, however, John sees a Lamb, standing as if it had been slaughtered. Of course, the point here is that God's victory is won through suffering and his triumph is achieved through sacrifice. The Lamb is indeed as powerful as a Lion, but his power is exercised through what he suffers for the sake of others.

- Contrary to what some modern readers may think, John was not writing in code. His word pictures do not attempt to conceal the identity of Jesus by picturing him as a Lamb but to reveal Jesus's character. In Revelation, Jesus is the messianic Lion, who exercises his power by dying for others, like a sacrificial Lamb.

- The Lamb is worthy to open God's scroll because it was by his blood that he purchased people of every tribe and nation and made them into a kingdom and priests who serve God. In other words, God's kingdom is built through the self-giving of Jesus. This is the way the Lamb "conquers," and for John, this is a worthy exercise of power.

The Four Horsemen

- The horsemen who appear as the Lamb starts to open the seals on God's scroll depict threats to the prevailing order. They challenge the complacency of those who think that current social, political, and economic conditions are their best source of security, for in John's mind, they are not.

Dürer's woodcuts—especially "The Four Riders of the Apocalypse"— are probably the most famous illustrations of Revelation ever made.

- The first horseman holds a bow and is given a crown, signifying victory, yet he is not a Roman soldier. He looks more like one of the tribal warriors who lived outside the borders of the empire and remained unconquered. This figure offers a disturbing reminder that a society created through conquest can be destroyed in the same way.

- The second horseman holds a great sword and is allowed to take peace from the earth. This rider challenges the prevailing attitude that the people conquered by Rome should be grateful to the empire for ensuring peace. For John, the rhetoric of peace espoused by the Romans concealed violence that worked below the surface.

- The third horseman holds a pair of scales, like those used in commerce. He also challenges the rhetoric of the time, which maintained that Roman rule had made life better than ever before. The third horseman heralds a food shortage and offers a vivid reminder about the limits of an economic system to guarantee prosperity.

- The fourth horseman represents death and is followed by a figure called Hades, the Greek name for the realm of the dead. This horseman pushes beyond threats of conquest, violence, and hardship to the power of death that threatens both rich and poor in countless ways.

The Threat of Injustice and the Coming Judgment

- When the Lamb opens the fifth seal, John sees a vision of martyrs, the victims of violence and injustice. The martyrs cry out, asking how long God will delay in taking action against a world in which the innocent suffer at the hands of the powerful. They call readers to see the faithful who suffer while the world turns a blind eye to violence.

- Like the other visions, this one raises questions about the readers' most basic commitments. Having heard the vulnerable calling for justice, will the readers identify with them, or will they, like so many others in society, turn away?

- To press the issue further, the Lamb opens the sixth seal, which brings the series to a climax with the most ominous picture thus far. As if in response to the victims' cry for justice, John pictures Creation itself giving signs of God's coming judgment.

- The sun becomes black as sackcloth, and the moon turns red as blood. The ground shakes, and people of every social class shake with it at the prospect of facing the justice of God. The vision warns that there is a higher authority to which even those at the pinnacle of society will be held accountable.

A Vision of Hope

- At this point in the book, John's word pictures have warned readers that a society created by conquest and violence can be destroyed through those same forces and that turning a blind eye to the victims of injustice will ultimately mean confronting the justice of God.

- Now, instead of continuing the onslaught of disturbing pictures, John offers his readers a vision of hope. Before the final seal is opened, we are transported back to the heavenly throne room, in the presence of the Creator and the Lamb.

- In the vision, John's initial understanding was that God planned to seal and protect 144,000 people who come from the 12 tribes of Israel. But when he turns to look at this group, he sees instead a countless multitude from every tribe and nation, a multitude redeemed by the Lamb to stand before God.

- This interplay of disturbing and inspiring word pictures is a key to how the Apocalypse works. The images move in cycles, with the author taking us through scenes that threaten us and into a vision of something hopeful and life-giving. That more hopeful vision is where the author wants his readers to arrive.

- The word pictures of Revelation grab our attention and draw us into the work, helping us to see things in new ways. They do not simply dispense bits of information for us to absorb but engage the imagination and stimulate our thoughts, bringing us into a process of reflection.

Suggested Reading

Aune, "The Influence of Roman Court Ceremonial on the Apocalypse of John."

Bauckham, *The Theology of the Book of Revelation*, pp. 31–53, 73–80.

Questions to Consider

1. Revelation conveys the character of God and Jesus through descriptions of the heavenly throne room and the slaughtered and living Lamb. What can such picture language do that an analytical treatment of God's character or Jesus's identity would not do? What are the limitations of such picture language?

2. The seven seals are linked to word pictures that challenge Roman claims to have established dominion through conquest, to provide secure peace, or to guarantee prosperity. The vision of the martyrs gives voice to the victims of injustice. Some of John's intended readers were suffering local harassment or persecution. How might they have responded to these visionary challenges to Roman claims? Other readers were prosperous and complacent under Roman rule. How might they have responded to these visions?

Seven Trumpets, Temple, and Celebration
Lecture 7

In this lecture, we look at the visions of the seven trumpets, in chapters 8–11 of Revelation, from two contrasting perspectives. First, we'll explore how people read these passages from a futuristic perspective, as if Revelation were a series of predictions about future events. Then, we'll see how this same section looks if we read it from a modern literary perspective, with the idea that Revelation is a piece of literature that uses vivid picture language to convey something about God's way of dealing with the world.

The Futuristic Perspective
- Some interpretations of Revelation assume that John is predicting a series of coming disasters in much the same way that weather forecasters predict the strength and path of a hurricane. In both situations, people are warned to prepare for the coming of inevitable devastation.

- Some people who read Revelation from this perspective believe that these disastrous events are still in the future, while others think that they have already started to take place and we are nearing the end of the world.

The Trumpet Visions
- In chapter 8 of Revelation, an angel stands beside the heavenly altar. The angel offers up the prayers of the saints before God, then hurls fire down onto the earth, signaling the onset of a series of plagues. Seven angels stand at the ready, holding seven trumpets in their hands. As each trumpet is blown, the horrors multiply.

- The futuristic approach assumes that each trumpet can be equated with a particular event in time and space. Some have argued that the trumpet visions predicted events that began to unfold in the mid-20th century.

- The fiery vision brought on by the first angel is connected with World War II in a futuristic perspective. The hail and fire that fall from the sky are identified with the aerial bombings that occurred during the war, wreaking unprecedented devastation.

- When the second angel blows his trumpet, something like a great mountain, burning with fire, is thrown into the sea. A third of the sea is turned to blood, many ships are destroyed, and many sea creatures die. Some of the futuristic readings identify this fiery mountain with the mushroom clouds that arose following the nuclear blasts at Hiroshima and Nagasaki.

- When the third angel blows his trumpet, a star called Wormwood falls from heaven, embittering the waters of the earth and causing those who drink these waters to die. For many futuristic interpreters, this was what happened in 1986 with the meltdown of the nuclear reactor at Chernobyl in the former Soviet Union.

- When the fourth angel blows his trumpet, the sky becomes dark, and the light of the sun, moon, and stars is dimmed. According to the scenario we have been following, this would equate to the Gulf War. At the end of that war in 1991, Saddam Hussein set hundreds of oil wells on fire, darkening the sky with smoke.

- The trumpeting of the fifth angel causes demonic locusts to fly out of the underworld. These locusts have faces like human beings, teeth like lions, and the mysterious power to inflict pain using their tails. For some people, this is a vision of modern military helicopters, which have human pilots yet fly like insects and can shoot fire in combat.

- When the sixth angel blows his trumpet, there is conflict along the Euphrates River. An enormous army of demonic horses and riders slays one-third of the human race. According to some futuristic scenarios, this must be the war in Iraq, which lies along the Euphrates. The fire-breathing horses are said to be prophecies about modern tanks.

- The people who follow this script find everything unfolding with a kind of mechanical precision, bringing us to the moment when the seventh trumpet is about to blow, the signal that the end has come.

- Many people find it compelling to think that Revelation has predicted the horrors and chaos of our time. In the midst of our present difficulties and challenges, Revelation offers hope that God is in control and has a plan. This sense of divine control provides assurance that things are unfolding as they should.

The Literary Context of the Trumpet Visions
- Recall the throne room of God that we saw in our last lecture. It was there that the heavenly company declared that God was the Creator of all things; his essential identity is as the giver of life. Why, then, would God want to devastate the world he has made? From a literary perspective, we need to assume that God is on the side of life, not death.

- Recall, too, the vision of the seven seals, in one of which we hear the cries of the martyrs, those who have suffered unjustly because of their faith. They ask how long God will refrain from bringing justice for their deaths. From a literary perspective, that question of justice informs the vision of the seven trumpets.

Dürer's woodcut shows the angels with seven trumpets as they herald plague after plague upon the world.

- The trumpet visions offer a surprising answer to the question of how long God would delay in bringing justice against a wicked and sinful world. The visions tell us not how long justice will take, but why God has refrained from bringing a final judgment against the world.

- In fact, the visions show that sending plagues of wrath against the world is futile. The reason God has delayed in bringing final judgment is to provide space for his people to bear witness.

- In Revelation 8, the author seems to say, "Let me show you what an outpouring of divine wrath would look like," and he depicts plague after plague afflicting the wicked on earth from every side. As each trumpet blows, an onslaught of horror rains down, but after the sixth trumpet, what has changed?

- The answer is that nothing has changed in humanity's relationship to God or to one another. And if we think about it, why should anything change? Why should people turn to a God who seems bent on destroying the world? The trumpet visions reveal that God could send plagues of wrath against a sinful and wicked world, but such action would be ineffectual.

- After the six trumpets have blown, we expect the sound of the last trumpet to herald the final judgment on the world. John sees a mighty angel descending from heaven, with his face shining like the sun. The angel plants his feet on sea and land, and seven thunders begin to roar.

- It would seem that the end has come, but a voice from heaven interrupts the movement toward judgment, telling John not to record what the thunders are saying. Their message is not the one God wants to send.

- Instead, God makes space for a different way of communicating with the world. The angel in the vision gives John a scroll to eat and tells him to prophesy again. That will be the way God communicates with the world, through the prophetic witness of John and people like him.

- The readers of Revelation are not to be spectators, sitting on the sidelines and waiting for God to bring an end to the world. Those who are addressed by this book are to be engaged in speaking the truth and calling the world to honor the ways of the God who created it.

The Temple and the Witnesses

- In chapter 11 of the Apocalypse, John sees a temple in which true worship takes place, and he sees two prophets, dressed in sackcloth, bearing witness to the world.

- Some futuristic readers believe that this vision refers to a new temple to be built on the site of the original Jewish Temple in Jerusalem. But a literary approach to Revelation reads John's use of the word "temple" as a vivid metaphor for the worshiping community.

- With the prophetic witnesses, John creates a collage of images from the Bible to form a composite picture of authentic witness. He pieces together memories of Moses turning water into blood and the prophet Elijah closing up the sky. We see that authentic witness is a vocation of truth-telling, and this is the pattern of life to which John's readers are called.

- John's vision of the witnesses also includes the story of their deaths, a warning to readers that the nations of the world will not necessarily be delighted to receive their message. The hope of the witnesses is ultimately for resurrection, not for easy victory.

- When the seventh trumpet finally sounds, it does not bring disaster but celebration. A chorus of voices declares that "the kingdom of the world has become the kingdom of our Lord and of his Christ, and he will reign forever and ever." This is the vision of the future to which the readers are called—a vision of celebration of the reign of God.

Suggested Reading

Barr, "Doing Violence."

Bauckham, *The Climax of Prophecy*, pp. 238–283.

Questions to Consider

1. The lecture sketches out two different ways of reading the trumpet visions. What assumptions do people make when reading the visions futuristically? What assumptions do people make when reading the visions from a literary perspective?

2. What kind of effect might the futuristic reading of the trumpet plagues have on readers? How would a futuristic reading shape life in the present? Conversely, what kind of effect might the literary reading of the trumpet plagues have on readers? How would this alternative reading shape life in the present?

The Dragon and the Problem of Evil
Lecture 8

With this lecture, we come to some of the most dramatic images in Revelation, relating to its portrayal of evil. We will consider four major images, beginning in this lecture with Satan as a great dragon, hurled down from the sky to prowl the earth. In lectures to come, we'll turn to Satan's allies: a seven-headed beast from the sea, a cunning beast from the land, and Babylon the Harlot. A key to our reading about these forces of evil is the announcement of the heavenly chorus that the time has come "to destroy the destroyers of the earth." If God is the Creator and his will for the world is life, then he must defeat those destructive forces that threaten life.

Cosmic Conflict

- The story of the cosmic conflict between God and the destroyers of the earth begins in chapter 12 of Revelation, where the parts of good and evil are played by a woman and a dragon.

- As the chapter opens, John sees a woman who is about to give birth to the messianic child, the one who is to rule the nations. In front of the woman stands a seven-headed dragon that is waiting to devour the child at the moment he is born. The woman gives birth, but the dragon's plot is foiled, for the child is caught up to heaven and the woman flees to the wilderness for safety.

- At that moment, war breaks out in heaven. Michael the archangel appears to battle the satanic dragon. He and his angels defeat the dragon and hurl the devilish monster down to the earth.

- But the dragon is determined not to surrender; he makes one more futile attempt to destroy the woman by unleashing a torrent of water from his mouth. As the water gushes after the woman, threatening to overwhelm her, the earth itself comes to the rescue and opens its mouth to swallow the water.

- The dragon then sets off to vent his rage elsewhere—this time, by making war against the woman's many other children—those who keep the commandments of God and the testimony of Jesus.

1st-Century *Star Wars*

- Like the *Star Wars* series of films, Revelation gives us scenes of intergalactic warfare among hordes of extraterrestrial beings. Both *Star Wars* and Revelation also focus on the classic struggle between good and evil.

- Such stories are appealing because, unlike ordinary life, they offer us a clear-cut choice between good and evil. Further, they have a way of drawing us in to the action so that we are not just spectators. We find ourselves identifying with the characters who are trying to bring deliverance from the destructive powers.

- In the eyes of John, the author of Revelation, the Roman Empire itself was a destructive force at work in the world. The empire was the dominant culture, and it expanded its dominion by subjugating neighboring peoples and suppressing internal dissent. John's identification was not with this dominant culture but with the Christian community.

- For John, the creative power of God was different from the destructive capacity of the empire. In his eyes, the redemptive power of the Lamb's self-sacrifice was completely unlike the pretensions of the imperial court. Thus, in Revelation, John inverted a classic story of good versus evil so that it no longer supported the values and beliefs of the dominant culture.

Ancient Stories of Good versus Evil

- Historians have noted that Revelation's story of the woman and the dragon has a plotline that is similar to other stories of good versus evil that circulated in the ancient world. One of these is the Greek story of a woman named Leto, who became pregnant by the god Zeus.

- Leto's adversary was a ferocious snake-like dragon named Python, who tried to kill her to prevent the births of Zeus's children. When the children were born—Apollo and Artemis—they were given arrows as gifts, with which Apollo slew the dragon.

- In the dominant culture of Roman imperialism, the emperors stepped into the role of Apollo; they were the ones who overcame the forces of chaos represented by the dragon. Virgil, for example, compared the rise of Augustus to the birth of Apollo.

Dover Pictorial Archive.

Dürer's "The Woman Clothed with the Sun and the Seven-headed Dragon" captures John's vision in the opening of Revelation 1, in which a dragon awaits to devour the woman's messianic child at birth.

- But in John's eyes, the dragon is not the thing that threatens the empire, and the emperor is not the hero. John sees the destructive forces of the dragon operating within the empire, and he sees the emperor as the dragon's ally.

John's Telling of the Ancient Story

- In John's version of the story, the first scene is about a woman giving birth to a child in the presence of a dragon. This child is obviously not Apollo or Caesar but Jesus, who, John tells us, was born to rule the nations. The dragon wears seven royal diadems on its heads, revealing its own determination to rule the world.

- The opening scene in John's vision also tells us that the child escaped from the dragon and was taken to God's throne in heaven. This adds an intriguing dimension to Revelation's account: The Messiah escaped from the dragon by suffering death and being raised to life with God. In other words, the dragon tries to exercise its power by inflicting death on its rival, but the Messiah's power is exercised by suffering death and winning victory over it through resurrection.

- The woman who gives birth to the Messiah is identified by some interpreters as Mary, but others see her as a representative of the community of faith, which is threatened by the power of the dragon. She personifies the people of Israel, from whom the Messiah was born, and is forced to flee into the wilderness to escape the dragon, just as ancient Israel had to flee to escape from the pharaoh.

- John also tells us that this woman actually had many children, specifically, all who keep the commandments of God and hold onto the witness of Jesus. John's readers would have identified strongly with those children, but they still might have asked why they should keep the commandments if doing so put them at risk.

Satan's Expulsion from Heaven

- John's response to this question is found in the middle scene of the vision, which tells of Satan's expulsion from heaven. If John's readers feel like the woman in the story, living in a social wilderness and threatened by local dragons, then the middle scene is the one that will shape their understanding of the character of evil in the world and their response to it.

- John recognizes that it is easy to think of evil working relentlessly on earth because it is so powerful, but he turns this perception upside down. For John, evil seems relentless not because it is powerful, but because it is desperate and losing. And the best way to respond to evil is to resist it, knowing that it cannot win out in the end.

- Once the Messiah has been taken to God's throne, a war breaks out in heaven, led by the archangel Michael. Michael and his angels defeat Satan and throw him down to earth, so that he can no longer come before the throne of God. His base of operations is now severely limited.

- In the middle scene of Revelation 12, Satan has lost the war in heaven and is wounded and angry. Prowling the earth, he lashes out in frustrated rage, trying to do as much damage as he can in his newly confined circumstances. This is not a demonstration of his power but of the fact that his time is running out. The best response now is not to capitulate to evil but to resist, knowing that ultimate power belongs to God.

- John assumes that people order their lives with an eye to what they believe has ultimate place. The dragon personifies deception, brutality, arrogance, and injustice. It's easy to see why people might think those forces run the world and why they might respond by simply giving in and going along.

- John, however, recognizes that the forces of evil operate in part by trying to breed a cynical complacency about the world. He challenges the idea that destructive forces can have ultimate place by showing that the power of the Creator is superior to and different from that of the destroyers. He calls on his readers to give their allegiance to what gives life, not to capitulate to the forces that bring death.

- As soon as Michael and his angels eject Satan and his allies, the heavenly voices explain that this victory is won through the blood of the Lamb and the word of those who bear witness. As we've seen before, the Lamb conveys the sacrificial power of love that is given in the face of hatred, and where this love prevails, there is victory.

Suggested Reading

Murphy, *Fallen Is Babylon*, pp. 277–296.

van Henten, "Dragon Myth and Imperial Ideology in Revelation 12–13."

Questions to Consider

1. Cosmic battles between the forces of good and evil have been popular since antiquity. What are some of the modern films and literary works that portray cosmic battles? Why do people today continue to find these stories engaging? How might comparing these modern epics to the dragon vision in Revelation 12 be helpful? How might such a comparison not be helpful?

2. Revelation calls readers to resist evil rather than capitulate to it. This call for resistance is based on the conviction that evil does not reign supreme. The author says that evil is being defeated through Jesus's self-sacrifice and his followers' witness to truth (Revelation 12:11). How might this call for resistance have been heard by the earliest readers of the book? How might it sound to Christian communities today? Would such a call for resistance be of value for those outside the Christian community? If so, why? If not, why not?

The Beasts and Evil in the Political Sphere
Lecture 9

In our last lecture, we explored John's portrayal of Satan as a great red dragon, thrown down from heaven so that he now prowls the earth. In this lecture, we will see John's characterization of evil in political life through the images of two beasts: the beast from the sea, who works in the realm of politics, and the beast from the land, who supports the beast from the sea through religious and economic practices that serve the interests of the empire. As we analyze John's literary strategy in this section of Revelation, it's helpful to think of the types of political cartoons that we see in the newspaper every day. Like modern cartoonists, John uses certain conventional images to comment on serious issues in contemporary life.

The Beast from the Sea
- In chapter 13 of Revelation, John sees a seven-headed beast rising up from the sea. For John, this monster represents evil taking tangible political form.

- John tells us that this hideous beast was known for its ability to conquer, and he says that the beast had authority over people of every tribe and language and nation. These traits are remarkably like those with which the Romans identified themselves. The military conquests of the emperors, for example, were celebrated in literature and art.

- John sees that violent conquest is at the heart of the empire, but he does not believe that the power to subjugate other nations is worthy of praise. For John, the empire is a predatory beast.

- John also notices that the Roman rulers sometimes made war internally, against those who seemed noncompliant. Thus, the beast makes war on the saints and conquers them; with this vision, John seems to set the empire against the Christian community.

- As mentioned earlier, there was apparently no empire-wide persecution of Christians in the 1st century, but John's readers probably would have vividly remembered the persecution of the church under the emperor Nero in the aftermath of the great fire in Rome. Needing a scapegoat on which to blame the fire, the emperor unleashed a vicious campaign of violence against the Christian community.

- This persecution in Rome lies at the heart of Revelation's portrayal of the beast from the sea. It is a picture that takes seriously the empire's own claim to dominate through violence. In his portrayal of Roman imperial power as a predatory beast, John uses some familiar images of beasts, relying especially on the book of Daniel, whose author also uses animal imagery to portray imperialism.

- Revelation combines the traits of four horrifying creatures from Daniel, symbolizing four empires, into a composite portrait. All these beasts are really part of one great beast: the phenomenon of empire. By using the imagery of beasts in this vision, John is trying to disclose the character of the political forces of his time in much the same way that political cartoonists do in modern newspapers.

- John tells us that the beast had been slain yet was alive. This detail picks up on ancient rumors that the emperor Nero was not really dead but in hiding. Some believed not only that Nero was alive but that he would someday return and resume power in Rome. John uses this bit of pop culture to show us the evil that never goes away.

John's symbolic beasts portray the politics of his day much like the caricatures found in today's political cartoons.

- From a literary perspective, the beast is the opposite of the Lamb. In Revelation, the power of God is exercised through the Lamb, and the power of evil is exercised through the beast. And these two forms of power are different in kind. Like the beast, the Lamb has been slain yet lives. But where the Lamb rises from the dead to give life to others, the beast rises from the dead to inflict death on others.

- John also uses the word "conquer" for both the Lamb and the beast. But where the Lamb "conquers" by faithfully suffering death for the sake of others, the beast conquers by inflicting death on others in order to subjugate them. John's purpose in contrasting these two forms of power is to ask which will claim the loyalty of his readers: the redemptive power of God or the oppressive power of the dragon.

The Beast from the Land

- For John, worship is an expression of a person's basic commitments. It shows where people place their highest loyalties. In John's vision, the specific question at issue is whether one's highest loyalty belongs to the empire or to God, whose purposes might be different from those of the empire.

- The test case for this question in John's world was the imperial cult, which is promoted by the beast from the land. As we consider this monster, it's helpful again to think of political cartoons, because John's imagery is again strange and even humorous, yet he is making a serious critique of the religious life of his day.

- In John's time, local temples to various emperors were built throughout Asia Minor, and public festivals connected to these sanctuaries were held, during which people turned out in droves to celebrate Roman rule.

- The most active supporters of the imperial cult were the leading citizens of Asia, many of whom both held civic office and served on the city council. John caricatures these citizens by picturing them as a two-horned beast that looks like a lamb but speaks like a dragon. This combination was meant to serve as a warning about the danger that may lurk beneath a seemingly innocent exterior.

- John develops the picture of the beast through comic exaggeration. He pictures the beast hawking the wonders of the ruler cult and getting people involved in making a statue for the tyrannical monster from the sea. The citizens seem oblivious to the monster's horrible appearance, but to distract them even further, the beast from the land makes the statue speak.

- The point of the satire, of course, is that no amount of hocus-pocus can change what the monster really is. And for people to worship it means that their highest loyalty is being given to leaders known for brutality. Given that the beast from the sea looks like Nero, it is even a beast that is willing to threaten the followers of Jesus.

The Mark of the Beast
- Another detail in this vision further presses the issue of basic commitments: At a couple of points in Revelation, John says that those who belong to God have a seal on their foreheads bearing the names of God and the Lamb. The idea is that belonging to God and the Lamb is what gives them their identity.

- In this vision, people are being pressured into accepting the mark of the beast in order to do business in the marketplace. It is, thus, the empire that gives them their identity.

- John concludes this section with a riddle; he tells us that the mark of the beast consists of the beast's name and number—which is 666—and challenges us to figure out what that means.

- The riddle makes use of an ancient practice called "gematria," which equates letters with numerical values. Using this technique, the Hebrew letters for the name Nero Caesar add up to 666.

- Once readers figure out that the number is connected to the overall picture of a beast like Nero, it sharpens the essential question John is asking: Whom do you belong to? What gives you your identity? God or the empire? The Lamb or the beast?

Suggested Reading

Bauckham, *The Climax of Prophecy*, pp. 384–452 ("Nero and the Beast").

Friesen, "The Beast from the Land."

Questions to Consider

1. The earliest readers of Revelation had different experiences under Roman rule. How might readers who were threatened with imprisonment have responded to the portrayal of imperial authority as a beast? How might the affluent readers who were prospering under Roman rule have reacted to this picture? How might the readers who wondered about the extent to which they could assimilate into Roman society have reacted?

2. The image of the beast presents the New Testament's most critical appraisal of Roman authority. Why might it be important to note that some New Testament voices were more positive about the authority of the state? Why might it be important to continue listening to Revelation's more critical view?

The Harlot and the Imperial Economy
Lecture 10

In the last lecture, we looked in detail at the beasts from the sea and the land, two images that exemplified the destructive evil present in the political and religious practices of John's society. In this lecture, we turn to Babylon, the prostitute who characterizes a city. As we focus on this image, we'll ask how John describes this figure and why there has been so much debate about what she symbolizes. From a literary perspective, we will also examine John's use of two forms of writing that are familiar to modern readers: satire, such as we might see in modern political cartoons, and the obituary.

Babylon the Harlot

- In the second half of Revelation, John is taken into a wilderness, where he sees a woman riding on the beast from the sea, John's image for Roman imperialism. She is harlot and represents the ultimate in materialism. John tells us that she is drunk with the blood of the saints and of the witnesses to Jesus.

- As the passage unfolds, it becomes clear that this woman symbolizes the city of Rome in its role of holding dominion over the world. She rides on the beast with seven heads, which represents seven kings and seven hills, a clear reference to the Seven Hills of Rome.

- When we read this vision from a literary perspective, two elements seem to stand out: conspicuous consumption and violence. The harlot is obviously obsessed with displays of wealth, and John's depiction of her stands as part of his critique of the craving for luxury and opulence in Roman society.

- In this passage, John also focuses on the kind of violence that had been experienced by Christians at Rome, and he later speaks about the violence the Romans perpetrated on other peoples through their campaigns of conquest.

- It's interesting that materialism and violence are linked to the image of a harlot, a supposedly seductive figure, but both can be seductive themselves. People often get a thrill and feel a sense of power from buying and owning expensive things, and they often experience a strange fascination with violence, as long as it doesn't become personal.

- The purpose of John's picture of the harlot is to startle readers into seeing the seductive qualities of materialism and brutality and then to change their perspective, so that what might appear alluring actually turns out to be repulsive. John wants his readers to resist these forces, to chart a different course that's based on different values.

John's Use of Satire
- As we've noted, John's word pictures often work in much the same way as modern political cartoons: by using well-known images to make sharp social critiques. Like modern cartoonists, John also uses satire to expose the shortcomings of society to the scrutiny of his readers. His portrait of Babylon would make readers wonder why anyone would want to conform to the values of Roman society.

- John's satire uses a template that is based on standard Roman imagery. A good example of this template is a picture found on a Roman coin from the late 1st century. In the center of the coin is the strong, graceful figure of the goddess Roma, who was the symbol of the city of Rome.

- John turns this picture into the image of a debauched prostitute. Instead of sitting calmly on the Seven Hills of Rome, John's version of Roma rides on a beast with seven heads. She no longer holds a sword gracefully in her hand but a goblet full of blood.

- It's also interesting to note that John changes the woman's name from Roma to Babylon in an effort to reveal something about her character. Giving her this name is a way of saying Roman society has the traits of Babylon, the capital of an empire remembered for its brutal conquests and its destruction of the Temple at Jerusalem.

- This grotesque image of the harlot is designed to challenge the perceptions of readers who thought that going along with the values of the imperial culture was perfectly acceptable. By creating this picture, John urges his readers to look beneath the surface and see the destructive currents at work in Roman society.

The Destruction of the Harlot

- To this point in the vision, John has been picturing society as a harlot who rides along in a drunken stupor on the back of the imperial beast. Next, he looks to the future, giving us a scene in which the beast destroys the harlot with fire and devours her flesh.

- This horrific scene offers one of Revelation's most pointed comments about the nature of evil: It is inherently self-destructive. John shows readers that the tendencies within society will come full circle, so that evil becomes evil's own undoing. His graphic word pictures show how a society that is enamored with the violence it can use against others may finally fall victim to violence itself.

- John does not want his readers to simply "go with the flow" of imperial culture, a point he makes explicit in Revelation 18:4. Here, a heavenly voice says, "Come out of her my people, so that you don't take part in her sins and don't receive any of her plagues." The call to "come out" of Babylon meant that readers were to reject destructive patterns and base their lives on different values.

- This message originally spoke about life in the imperial world, but it also gives modern readers something to ponder. The vision points to the seductive quality of wealth and what it means to be part of a culture of consumption. It also recognizes the fact that violence can be both alluring and mind-numbing.

Babylon's Funeral
- In chapter 18, John writes a unique kind of obituary for the harlot, showing us the people who mourn the collapse of Babylon. He gives special attention to the merchants, who are grieving the loss of the huge profits they made by selling their goods in the city. The more they lament the city's demise, the more we realize that what really matters to them is not the city but the money they've lost.

- As the merchants speak, they reflect a worldview in which everything has been turned into a commodity. They rattle off an incredible list of goods they could sell to Babylon at a hefty profit. Modern scholars looking at this list note that it depicts Rome as relentlessly gobbling up everything the world has to offer.

- In addition to gold and silver, jewels and pearls, fabrics, exotic wood, ivory, spices, iron, wheat, and bronze, the merchants also did a brisk business in slaves. For John, the slave trade represented the epitome of life in Babylon, a world in which everything had become a commodity, even human life.

- Of course, for John's readers, Roman society was still very much alive. But John writes this strange obituary of Rome to startle his readers into imagining what their society's legacy will be after their time is over.

- The 19th-century inventor of dynamite, Alfred Nobel, had the strange experience of reading his own obituary before his death and was deeply disturbed by the identification of his legacy as one of wealth and violence. He determined to commit himself to a different future by creating the Nobel prizes in science, medicine, literature, and peace. Revelation's obituary of Babylon is meant to have a similar effect.

Suggested Reading

Koester, "Roman Slave Trade and the Critique of Babylon in Revelation 18."

Kraybill, *Imperial Cult and Commerce in John's Apocalypse*.

Questions to Consider

1. Revelation's portrayal of Rome as a harlot is a form of satire that is comparable to modern political cartoons. Why might a modern commentator choose to critique social or political realities in a cartoon rather than in an ordinary editorial? What might make a satirical picture highly effective in some situations? What would make such a satirical picture ineffective?

2. The author of Revelation is sharply critical of the materialism and brutality he sees in Roman society. He warns that these same tendencies will ultimately destroy that society. Does Revelation's satirical picture of the harlot make the ancient writer's views clear to modern readers? What aspects of the picture might be confusing? What aspects of the picture might be compelling?

The Battle, the Kingdom, and Last Judgment
Lecture 11

In this lecture, we come to scenes in Revelation that have inspired both dread and fascination, scenes ranging from the great battle of Armageddon, to the final defeat of Satan, and the last judgment. These scenes mark the climax of God's battle against the forces of evil that have shaped the social, political, and economic life of society. In the aftermath, we learn how God will finally bring about divine justice for those who have suffered for their faith and how all of us be judged at the end of time.

The Site of Armageddon

- The idea that Armageddon is linked with current events in the Middle East is strongest among those who follow a futuristic approach to Revelation.

- According to a common futuristic theory, the battle of Armageddon will rage across northern Israel into central and southern Jordan. The battle will culminate with fierce fighting in and around the city of Jerusalem, where God will ultimately win.

- The word "Armageddon" is derived from two Hebrew words: "har," meaning a mountain or hill, and "Megiddo," which is the name of an ancient city in northern Israel.

- From a literary perspective, it seems clear that the author of Revelation used this name for its symbolic value. Megiddo was where the Canaanite armies met their demise in the early history of Israel and where some of the allies of the wicked Queen Jezebel were defeated. When the author of Revelation uses a form of this name, he is saying that this is the battleground where evil meets its Waterloo.

How the Battle Will Be Fought

- The Dead Sea Scrolls included a text called the War Scroll, which pictured a huge battle with thousands of warriors taking the field at the end of the age. According to the War Scroll, these vast armies carried iron swords, bronze shields, and spears. For many modern readers, that classic scenario has been updated to include the latest military technology, in particular, tanks, airplanes, and nuclear missiles.

- In Revelation, the battle actually begins when heaven is opened, and Christ appears on a white horse. His uniform consists of a robe that has been dipped in his own blood, a visible reminder of the blood he has already shed for the sake of others.

- How will Christ defeat the forces of evil that tyrannize the world? The one weapon he will use in this battle is the sword from his mouth, in other words, his word of truth. In the end, the battle of Armageddon is about the triumph of Christ's word.

- The losers in the battle are the seven-headed beast that personifies tyranny and the beast from the land that promotes the ruler cult. Recall that the seven-headed beast is John's image of a system of oppression. That system has the traits of empires gone by, along with those of imperial Rome.

- The beast from the land, or the false prophet, shows how the religious currents of the empire could be harnessed to support the oppressive system—by turning its leaders into gods. At Armageddon, these beast-like forces are finally stopped by the word that Christ speaks. The carnage that John describes is the carnage of a system of oppression being brought to an end when truth overpowers it.

The Aftermath of the Battle

- Armageddon culminates when Satan is captured and chained up by an angel, then banished to the abyss below the earth, where he is imprisoned for 1,000 years.

- When this sentence is over, Satan is released and goes right back to his old ways. He tricks the mysterious nations of Gog and Magog so that they mount one more futile attack against the reign of God.

- In a surprising anticlimax, fire simply comes down from heaven and ends the battle before it starts. Finally, Satan is thrown into a lake of fire and put out of business permanently.

- It's important to note that these scenes are not about destroying the earth but about destroying the destroyers of earth. God's goal is to liberate the world from the forces that diminish life.

- Also significant is the central role that God's truth plays in the battle. The scenes of Armageddon do not picture one group of human beings slaughtering another. Rather, they emphasize the power of Christ's path of sacrifice, symbolized by the robe stained with his own blood. The power of Christ's word brings tyranny and deception to an end.

- Finally, these scenes tell readers that God's purposes are ultimately on the side of justice and truth. Although experience might teach that the world is not fair, Revelation offers a vision in which justice wins out in the end.

Divine Justice for the Individual

- Thus far, we've focused on the way in which the justice of God brings broad systems of oppression to an end. What does this mean for individuals? Two scenes in Revelation 20 take up this question: the resurrection of the martyrs and the resurrection and final judgment of all people.

- At the beginning of Revelation 20, John tells us that he saw those who had been killed for their faith being raised to life again. This is an act of divine justice. After these martyrs are resurrected, they share in the blessings of Christ's kingdom during the 1,000-year period when Satan is imprisoned in the abyss.

- The last major scene in chapter 20 is the resurrection of all the dead for the last judgment. The prospect of this final judgment has had a profound impact on Christianity. One of the most famous depictions of it is that by Michelangelo behind the altar in the Sistine Chapel.

- Both Michelangelo's fresco and Revelation feature two books: the books of deeds and the book of life. In Revelation these books point to two main factors at work in the judgment scene: human accountability and divine grace.

© Photos.com/Getty Images/Thinkstock.

The prospect of a final judgment has had a profound impact on Christianity. Many artists have tried to capture the sense of it on a grand scale.

The Books of Deeds

- An ancient tradition held that a king could have the notable actions of his people recorded in a book. Later, this idea developed into the notion that all of our deeds are written down in heavenly books. According to Daniel, these books are to be opened at the last judgment.

- The idea promoted by these books is that human actions matter to God. God's role here is important because experience teaches us that all too often, some people get away with destructive or hurtful deeds at the expense of others. At the same time, our positive actions sometimes go unnoticed.

- Ultimately, being accountable to God means that people are called to something higher than the approval we get from others. This gives us incentive to do what is right, even if no one else seems to notice, and it strengthens the conviction that injustice will not win out in the end.

- The downside of this notion of divine judgment is that it leaves us with an image of God as a heavenly scorekeeper. This is where the book of life, signifying divine grace, enters the picture.

The Book of Life

- The idea of the book of life originally comes from the Hebrew Bible, where it referred to those who are currently living. As the prophetic tradition developed into the apocalyptic tradition, the idea expanded to include the hope of resurrection. Thus, the book of life came to represent the promise of everlasting life.

- In a sense, the book of life was like the official list of citizens kept by some cities. In Revelation, the book of life is the register of people who will live as citizens of New Jerusalem, the city that people enter by way of resurrection to life everlasting.

- According to Revelation, people are written into the book of life from the foundation of the world, not because they have done a certain number of good deeds. Because their names are written in the book from the start, then God must have decided to include them as an act of divine favor. Ultimately, this book of life—this act of grace—is what carries weight in the last judgment.

- It seems as if God has arbitrarily picked some people for eternal life and not others, but this interpretation makes God look like a tyrant and seems to contradict the scenes of hope in Revelation.

- The inclusion of both the book of life and the books of deeds in the judgment scene represents a paradox in Revelation: People are accountable for what they do, yet they are not saved by what they do; they are saved by the grace of God.

- Our actions affect the people around us, and that's why our actions matter. Yet in the final analysis, Revelation assumes that the future can only be a gift from the Creator, whose purposes will culminate in making all things new.

Suggested Reading

Boring, *Revelation*, pp. 194–213.

Stylianopoulios, "I Know your Works."

Questions to Consider

1. Revelation transforms the language of warfare by picturing a battle in which the one weapon used is the word. Rather than picturing a war that destroys the world, the book depicts a conflict that frees the world from the powers that now destroy it. In what ways does this distinctive battle imagery offer a compelling sense of hope to readers facing social and political evils? In what ways might this imagery be problematic?

2. Revelation, like other New Testament writings, expects a final judgment in which people are held accountable to God. What effect might this belief have had on the early readers who were undergoing harassment or persecution? What effect might it have had on readers who were comfortable with the social, political, and religious practices of the imperial world?

New Creation and New Jerusalem
Lecture 12

I n the final scene of Revelation, we see John's visions of a new heaven and a new earth and of New Jerusalem, the city of God, descending from heaven in splendor. A voice announces that God has come to dwell with people. Death is gone, and the age of sorrow is over. The scene is an explosion of light and color, but depictions of it in popular culture are often more entertaining than compelling. In this lecture, we'll focus not on the details of the New Jerusalem passage, such as the pearly gates or the streets paved with gold, but on the larger cosmic, social, political, and sacred dimensions of the scene. We will close this section of the course by asking what kind of invitation this climactic scene offers to readers.

Cosmic Dimensions of New Jerusalem

- The popular pictures of heaven often focus on where individuals go when they die, but in the last scene of Revelation, we are given a picture of a new creation. The author doesn't separate the future of the individual from the future of the world. He takes the two together, and the result is breathtaking.

- John sees an essential consistency in the work of God as the Creator. Throughout Revelation, we have seen that God's nature is life-giving, and the goal of his work in destroying the forces of evil has been this final act of new creation. Death itself has been overthrown, and what remains is life.

- In this last scene, God says, "Behold, I am making all things new!" These words can be read as both a promise and a challenge. The promise that God makes "all things new" tells readers that the scale of God's action is cosmic and that his goal is transformative.

- But if readers see that as the commitment of God, how are their own commitments affected? And what are the practical implications of that hope for life in the present?

Social Dimensions of New Jerusalem

- It's significant that Revelation's last chapters portray a city, because in the ancient world, the city was one of the most important sources of identity and belonging for an individual outside of the family. John is not offering readers their own private heaven but a community in which they can participate.

- Earlier, we saw John's picture of Babylon as a harlot. Applying this image more broadly to society, John shows us what happens when pleasure and profit become the ultimate values. Life becomes degraded, and society ultimately destroys itself.

- John uses the opposite image for New Jerusalem, picturing the city as a bride. For readers of his time, the bridal imagery would have conveyed values that centered on faithfulness and commitment. Here, John is reaching back to the tradition of the Hebrew prophets, who had pictured Israel's covenant with God as a marriage.

- According to the prophets, Israel was the bride and God was the husband, and the sense of commitment went both ways. God made it clear that he wanted to be in a relationship with Israel and that he would be faithful to these people.

- Early Christians extended this imagery by referring to Jesus as the bridegroom, and Revelation follows this pattern by calling New Jerusalem the bride of the Lamb. The author previously referred to Jesus as the faithful witness and called Jesus the one who acts faithfully. Those who follow him as his bride are called to the same path of fidelity and commitment.

- Revelation uses the image of the bride to define a way of life that is different from the self-absorbed ways of the harlot and her clients. Earlier, John showed us that the destructive forces Babylon used against others would eventually destroy Babylon itself. But the bride that is New Jerusalem has a future, and in light of that future, readers are called to follow the ways of the bride in the present.

Political Dimensions of New Jerusalem

- The cities where the early readers of Revelation lived were monuments to human achievement, with structures that expressed the greatness of their ancient rulers. Such cities as Ephesus, Smyrna, and Pergamum had massive city walls with huge gates. These and other urban monuments often included inscriptions dedicating the structures to those in power.

- The New Jerusalem of John's vision reflects a different kind of power structure. The imagery here is fantastic and even outlandish, but the point is to push the human imagination to its limits and beyond, to show that the city of God can never be equated with any earthly city.

- The qualities of the city John describes are mind-boggling. It measures 1,500 miles on each side and is 1,500 miles high; its streets are paved with gold. The inscriptions over the gates of New Jerusalem bear the names not of emperors or local deities but of the tribes of Israel. Those on the city's foundations bear the names of the apostles of the Lamb.

- This story of alternative authority is reflected in part in the city's name. John's early readers would have identified Jerusalem with the history of Israel and with the time of Jesus on earth. But by the 1st century, much of historic Jerusalem had been destroyed in the Jewish revolt against Rome, and the future of the city was uncertain. The vision of New Jerusalem reiterates the idea that God's purposes cannot be equated with any earthly city, even Jerusalem itself.

- It's clear from the vision of New Jerusalem that God's designs go beyond a simple restoration of the old order of things. The city descends from heaven rather than being built up from earth, and its splendor goes beyond even the most fantastic hopes of the Hebrew prophets.

Sacred Dimensions of New Jerusalem

- John's description of New Jerusalem includes an intriguing detail: He says that he saw no temple in the city, for its temple is the Lord God Almighty and the Lamb.

- For ancient readers, a temple was essential to life in the city. Ephesus, for example, was famous for its temple to the goddess Artemis, and Pergamum was known for its temple to the emperor Augustus.

- The importance of a temple was also present in Israel's tradition, but the Jewish people had only one temple because there was only one God. The Jewish Temple in Jerusalem had been destroyed by the Romans in 70 A.D. in their efforts to suppress the revolt.

- In the wake of this disaster, we might have expected John to promise that a new temple would be built in the New Jerusalem. But in John's vision, the entire notion of a temple is transformed.

- The idea behind a temple is that it is a place set apart for God, but in New Jerusalem, there is no longer any barrier between God and human beings. For people to worship in the "temple" is simply to worship in the presence of the God who made them and the Lamb who frees them. From this perspective, New Jerusalem is the relationship of God and humanity made whole.

The Invitation into God's Future

- One of the details of New Jerusalem that people often pick up on is the pearly gates. But the conventional picture of the pearly gates is actually the opposite of what we find in Revelation.

- The New Jerusalem in Revelation is a city with 12 gates, all of which stand open all the time. The gates exist not to keep people out but to invite them in, because this city is where God wants people to be.

Lecture 12: New Creation and New Jerusalem

- John's vision is not limited to an individual here or there showing up at the pearly gates. He reaches back to the most expansive passages in the Hebrew prophets, which picture the nations of the world streaming into New Jerusalem, all invited to pursue the life that God intends.

- The breadth of the vision continues right up to the end, where John brings the readers to the tree of life. Of course, the tree of life was first mentioned in Genesis. When God expelled Adam and Eve from the Garden of Eden, they could no longer take fruit from the tree of life and live forever. But in the New Jerusalem, God opens up a way to life that sin had closed off.

- These visions of hope invite people into a future that is characterized by life, just as the many disturbing visions that we've seen seek to move people away from the destructive patterns that so often dominate our lives in the present. It is this interplay between promise and warning that is designed to move readers to a renewed engagement with the life-giving ways of God.

Suggested Reading

Bauckham, *The Theology of the Book of Revelation*.

Rossing, *The Choice between Two Cities*.

Questions to Consider

1. Revelation contrasts two cities: Babylon signifies the materialism and brutality of the Roman world; New Jerusalem is the future world of life and peace in the presence of God. What might the contrast between Babylon and New Jerusalem have meant to early Christians who faced harassment and persecution? What might the contrast have meant to those who were prosperous and complacent?

2. Revelation culminates in a vision of a new creation, where the tree of life bears fruit for all and the river of life flows through God's city. How might this vision of the future world lead readers to devalue the present world? How might this same vision lead readers to renewed appreciation of the present world?

Antichrist and the Millennium
Lecture 13

In this third section of the course, we will explore what happened after the book of Revelation was written and why it has managed to generate so much debate in Western society over the past 2,000 years. A point to keep in mind as we move through this sweep of Western history is that much of what people have seen in Revelation depends on the assumptions they make and the questions they ask. For example, some readers assume that Revelation provides a literal outline of events leading up to the end of the age, which leads them to ask how much it can tell them about the future. Others assume that the book uses spiritual imagery, which prompts questions about what the book might mean for spiritual life in the present. In this lecture, we'll see how these different sets of assumptions clashed with each other in the ancient world.

Topics of Interest in the Early Church

- The Antichrist and the millennium are two topics that played a major role in debates about Revelation in the 2nd and 3rd centuries A.D. The Antichrist is the name given to an evil figure who was expected to arise at some point in the future. The millennium was the 1,000-year period of peace expected to occur after the end of the present age.

- The debates about the Antichrist and the millennium arose out of basic questions about evil and hope. Like someone diagnosed with cancer, people who reflected on these topics were trying to develop tangible answers to basic questions: Just what do we need to be afraid of, and what can we hope for in the future?

The Antichrist

- In the 2nd and 3rd centuries, the Apocalypse circulated outside of Asia Minor and reached Christians farther to the west. One of these Christians was Irenaeus, the bishop of Lyons, who addressed the question of the Antichrist in his book *Against Heresies*.

- The other key thinker we will discuss was Hippolytus, a leading figure of the church in Rome. Hippolytus wrote a treatise called "On Christ and Antichrist" that influenced many later thinkers.

- Both of these writers assumed that Revelation had been written by John the apostle, and they used the book as an important source for their theological writings. Both also sought to discern what the role of evil might be in the future and concluded that the future would be a time of conflict.

- Irenaeus and Hippolytus combined elements from numerous books of the Bible into a new synthesis. The composite picture they created included the beast from Revelation and the man of lawlessness from Second Thessalonians. The term "Antichrist" came from the epistles of First and Second John.

- We've noted that the seven-headed beast in Revelation was an image of Roman imperialism, but Irenaeus and Hippolytus interpreted it as a tyrannical individual. When they read about the beast conquering the nations and persecuting the followers of Jesus, they took it as a prediction about a particular tyrant who would come in the future to oppress the world.

- Like the beast of Revelation, the man of lawlessness from Second Thessalonians is an agent of Satan, and he also becomes an object of worship. Revelation used the image of the beast of the land to critique the Roman imperial cult, but in Second Thessalonians, the man of lawlessness takes over the temple of God, which was Israel's temple.

- Of course, the Jerusalem Temple had been destroyed more than a century before the time of Irenaeus and Hippolytus, but Hippolytus concluded that the Antichrist would have to rebuild the temple so that he could enter it. From that time down to the present, many people have looked for a new temple to be built in Jerusalem to enable the completion of prophetic history.

- The name "Antichrist" is not used in Revelation but only in the letters of First and Second John. There, the term refers to people who had been part of the Christian community, but who came to embrace a form of the faith that denied the importance of Jesus's humanity. For the author of First John, those who abandon the belief in a truly human Jesus have become "anti-Christ."

The Picture of Irenaeus and Hippolytus

- For Irenaeus and Hippolytus, the beast is no longer a symbol of Roman imperialism, and the Antichrist is no longer a title for those who have embraced an overly spiritualized form of Christianity. Rather, the picture is of an individual tyrant who will be the agent of Satan at the end of the age.

- The end will be a time of conflict, during which the Antichrist enters the rebuilt temple to announce his own divinity. When Christians resist, the Antichrist will unleash a terrible persecution, which will end with the Second Coming of Christ.

- This picture of the Antichrist became standard and has appeared in writings of the Middle Ages down to the present. Possible candidates have included the pope, Napoleon, and Adolf Hitler.

- This tradition of the Antichrist has fueled speculation about the future that seems unhelpful and hurtful. It is perhaps more useful to explore the question posed by Irenaeus and Hippolytus, rather than their answer. These thinkers were trying to formulate a tangible sense of evil and its future.

The Millennium

- Ironically, the meaning of the millennium—the 1,000-year period of peace that many Christians have expected to occur at the end of the age—has also been a source of major conflict. The issue centers on the interpretation of several verses near the end of the Apocalypse that describe the saints reigning with Christ for 1,000 years.

- Some Christians thought the passage referred to a literal 1,000 years of peace and prosperity on earth. Others were emphatic that it did not have this meaning and was a purely spiritual reality. The debate was so divisive that it nearly led to Revelation being kept out of the New Testament.

- The origins of the dispute can be traced back to Irenaeus. His overall assumption was that the world would endure for 6,000 years, after which there would be a seventh period of peace and rest—Revelation's vision of the 1,000-year reign of the saints.

To Irenaeus and Hippolytus, the Antichrist came to signify an individual tyrant who would be Satan's agent at the end of the age—someone such as Hitler.

- Revelation 20:4–6 is the place where two lines of the plot overlap. In terms of the book's literary structure, the 1,000-year period is a transitional point, when Satan is bound but not gone, and the resurrection has started but is not yet finished.

- Many early Christians inferred that the passage referred to a literal kingdom on earth. They began filling in the details by connecting these cryptic verses of Revelation with other parts of the Bible. Justin Martyr, for example, who wrote in the 2nd century A.D., equated Revelation's millennial kingdom with Isaiah 65.

- Irenaeus's belief in the justice of God led him to insist that the millennial kingdom would be an earthly one. Given that people had been killed on earth for their faith, he believed that God would give them new life on earth and restore Creation to a condition of perfection so that those who had suffered could enjoy its bounty.

- Unlike the Gnostics, who taught that the material world was inherently evil, Irenaeus was also committed to the idea that God's Creation was good. He was convinced that God would redeem not just human souls but the world itself.

Opposition to Irenaeus

- The center of opposition to Irenaeus was the city of Alexandria in Egypt. Many Christians there valued philosophy and favored a spiritual reading of biblical texts, including Revelation.

- According to the Alexandrian tradition, the earthly images in the text pointed to higher spiritual meanings. As these Christians read the Bible, they sought to learn how its message promoted a life of virtue, what it said about spiritual discipline, and how it might shape the lives of believers and the church as a whole.

- When the Alexandrians came across the more lavish descriptions of the earthly millennial kingdom, they were shocked at the bodily indulgence such descriptions seemed to encourage. The bishop of Alexandria, Dionysius, critiqued not only the futuristic interpretation of Revelation but the book itself, arguing that it had not been written by the apostle John.

- This had the effect of moving the book out to the margin of what was acceptable for Christians in the eastern Roman Empire and causing tension between the east and the west. Christians in the west tended to value Revelation highly, while those in the east were dubious.

- John's description of the millennial kingdom in Revelation 20 does not fit easily into the ordinary realm of time and space. As we've said repeatedly, what his vision does offer is a clear sense that the purposes of God are ultimately directed toward life.

Hill, *Regnum Caelorum*.

McGinn, *Antichrist*, pp. 1–63.

1. The ancient discussion about the Antichrist was a response to the problem of evil. What problems might arise when people try to picture evil in a manner that is so specific and tangible? What problems might arise when people allow the notion of evil to remain general and abstract?

2. The early church's fascination with the vision of the 1,000-year reign of the saints was a response to questions about hope for the Creation and hope for justice. What problems might arise when hope for the world and society take such a specific and tangible form? What problems might arise when hope for the world remains general and abstract?

Revelation's Place in the Christian Bible
Lecture 14

How did the book of Revelation—the interpretation of which is disputed even today—ever find a place in the New Testament? In this lecture, we'll explore the canonical process, meaning the process that led to the formation of this normative collection of sacred writings. We'll look at several examples of other apocalyptic writings that had significant status in the early church, along with some early Christian controversies, to try to discover why Revelation was the one apocalypse to be included in the Christian canon.

Identifying Canonical Texts

- The earliest Christian communities were fairly small and had their own local leadership, with no centralized authority. Membership in these communities was entirely voluntary. Those who found Christian beliefs compelling could affiliate, but others had no reason to do so.

- The geographical diffusion of the early Christian communities compounded the complexity of maintaining a sense of Christian identity over time and space. The early Christians needed a sense of clarity about the beliefs that held them together, which included identifying their canonical texts.

- Many of the writings that early Christians used to identify their basic beliefs were Scriptures inherited from Judaism, such as the Torah, the prophetic texts, and the Psalms and other writings. Early Christians also produced their own texts, including the letters of Paul, various accounts of Jesus's life and ministry, and apocalyptic texts.

- Given that numerous apocalypses were in circulation in the 2nd and 3rd centuries, how is it that Revelation was given special status? To answer this question, we consider three apocalypses that were highly valued and their roles in the canonical process.

Fourth Ezra or Second Esdras

- The book known as Fourth Ezra or Second Esdras is a Jewish apocalypse written near the end of the 1st century. This text has traditionally been printed as an appendix to the Latin Bible and in the section known as the Apocrypha in many English translations of the Bible.

- The writer of Fourth Ezra, living in the time after the destruction of the second Jewish Temple by the Romans, begins by asking why God allowed Jerusalem to be destroyed. Although the people of Israel may be sinful, those who conquered the city are certainly no better.

- An angel appears to Ezra and tells him that his understanding of God's justice is far too limited. The angel says that at the end of the age, God's purposes will be achieved. Then, the apocalypse includes a vision of the arrival of the Messiah and his kingdom, followed by the final resurrection and last judgment.

- With this emphasis on God's justice, the book of Fourth Ezra has some similarities to Revelation. We also see similarities in the use of word pictures. Revelation pictures the community of faith as the woman who fled from the dragon, and the writer of Fourth Ezra pictures Jerusalem as a woman in grief.

- However, Fourth Ezra pictures the Messiah only as a victorious lion, not as a slaughtered Lamb. In this, it lacks Revelation's sense of paradox and neglects the idea that the Messiah's self-sacrifice is integral to God's way of working in the world.

- Although Fourth Ezra was written by a Jewish author, it was given greater value by the Christian community, probably because of its interest in the mystery of suffering and the Messiah's victory. Still, the book wasn't given full authority because it did not have a long and venerable tradition of usage.

The Apocalypse of Peter

- The Apocalypse of Peter was written by a Christian author in the early 2nd century. The writer identifies himself as the apostle Peter, but scholars agree that this was a pen name.

- This apocalypse offers a lurid vision of the horrors awaiting the wicked in the next world and promises a beautiful kingdom to the righteous. The message here is quite clear: Sin brings horrific punishment, whereas godly living brings wondrous rewards.

- Some early Christians, such as the author of the Muratorian Canon, thought that the Apocalypse of Peter should be given authoritative status. Others, however, rejected the book. The ancient church historian Eusebius noted that recognized teachers of the faith had not used the Apocalypse of Peter, and this lack of usage showed a consensus that the book did not warrant special status.

The Shepherd of Hermas

- Hermas writes as a Christian prophet and does not claim apostolic authority. This author tells us that in former times, he had been a slave and was later set free by the woman who bought him. The focus of his apocalypse is on sin and repentance.

- As the story begins, Hermas feels the pull of temptation. He has a vision of the woman who used to be his owner as she is bathing in the Tiber River. In the next vision, the woman accuses Hermas of having wicked and lustful thoughts, prompting him to ask how he might receive forgiveness.

- As the book continues, the question of sin and repentance is expanded. There is a vision of an elderly woman who gives Hermas a book, from which he learns that for the time being, God will allow people to repent of their sins. But he is warned that in the future, the time for repentance will end and people will be judged.

- The Shepherd of Hermas was widely read in the 2nd and 3rd centuries and included in one of the most important ancient manuscripts of the New Testament, the Codex Sinaiticus. But some early Christians argued that Hermas could not be put on the same level as other New Testament books, primarily because it had been written too long after the time of the apostles.

Christian Controversies
- As this process of identifying canonical texts was taking place, certain controversies gave special intensity to the place of apocalyptic writings in the church.

- The main challenge came from the followers of a man named Montanus, who lived in the 2nd century A.D. and claimed to have special prophetic inspiration. Montanus thought that a new age was dawning and that the world was on the verge of a fresh outpouring of the Holy Spirit. One of his followers declared that the New Jerusalem would soon come to earth at the city of Pepuza in Phrygia.

- One of the leading opponents of Montanism was a church leader named Gaius. To discredit the Montanists, Gaius attacked Revelation, which seemed to be fueling the apocalyptic movement. According to Gaius, Revelation had been written by a notorious heretic, and people were attracted to the idea of the 1,000-year kingdom because they saw it as a place where they could indulge their lust for bodily pleasure.

- People in the west generally did not listen to Gaius, and by the 4th century, even Christians in the east began to accept the idea that Revelation was an authoritative text. In the mid-4th century, the bishop of Alexandria, Athanasius, included Revelation in his list of books that were authoritative for the Christian community.

Forming a Consensus
- The formation of a consensus on the Christian canon grew out of the interplay of at least three factors. To be considered for inclusion, a text had to preserve apostolic teaching, its message had to be congruent with the teaching of the church, and it had to have a long and wide history of usage in the church.

- Early Christians gave considerable weight to books they thought were written by one of the apostles, but they did not insist an apostolic authorship. Further, if a claim was made that a book was written by an apostle, but its message seemed to depart from the traditional teaching of the church, the book would not be considered apostolic.

- The second criterion for inclusion in the canon was that the book in question had to be congruent with the teaching of the church. In the case of Revelation, Irenaeus used quotations from the book to affirm certain key Christian beliefs: that God was the Creator, who was made known through the Scriptures of Israel, and that Jesus was the Messiah whom the Scriptures had promised.

- The third criterion for inclusion was that the book had to have been widely used in the church; no individual could simply decree which books were authoritative.

- Under these criteria, Revelation was eventually recognized as one of the texts that could be shared as normative by most Christians. Its inclusion in the canon did not end the debates about how Revelation was to be interpreted but provided a focus for the discussion.

deSilva, "2 Esdras: The Mighty One Has Not Forgotten."

McDonald, *The Formation of the Christian Biblical Canon.*

Questions to Consider

1. This lecture summarized the main themes of three apocalypses that were popular in the early church but are not in the New Testament. Which of these would you find most interesting to read for yourself? Based on your impressions thus far, how do these writings seem similar to the book of Revelation? What aspects seem different?

2. Revelation was widely read in the 2nd century, but major questions about the book arose because some thought it encouraged too much speculation about the future and fueled the idea that the end of the age was at hand. To what extent are these ancient concerns like those that people have about Revelation today? In what ways might concerns about Revelation be different now than they were in the early church?

The Apocalypse and Spiritual Life
Lecture 15

In this section of the course, we are looking at the impact Revelation has had in Western culture and some of the debates it has sparked. As we've noted, much in these debates depends on the assumptions people make about the book and the questions they ask of it. Interpreters who assume that the book provides glimpses of coming events, for example, ask how those events will play out in the future. Others who assume that the book uses symbolic language to convey spiritual truths want to know what it says about each person's relationship to God in the present. In this lecture, we'll take up three topics—symbolism in Revelation, internal repetitions in the book, and its sense of time—that influenced the idea of a spiritual reading of Revelation that became dominant by the 4th and 5th centuries.

The Question of Symbolism

- If there is anything that divides readers of Revelation it is the question of how to interpret the book's symbolism. Still today, many people insist that the book is to be interpreted as literally as possible, but even the most literalistic interpreters recognize that Revelation uses symbolic language. Everyone agrees, for example, that the image of the beast is symbolic; at issue is what the symbolism means.

Plato greatly influenced Origen's interpretation of the Bible.

- In the ancient church, one of the interpreters who reveled in the symbolism of Revelation was Origen, a 3rd-century philosopher and biblical thinker. His reading of the Bible was shaped by the teachings of Plato.

- Platonic philosophy had a special interest in the transcendent realm of ideas, which was accessible through the mind. The counterpart to this was the visible world in which people lived; things in this world were accessible through the senses, but all material things were mere shadows of what existed in the higher world above. Origen was most interested in the transcendent world, which for him, was the eternal world of God.

- Origen thought of the Bible as a book with several levels of meaning: literal, moral, and spiritual. He valued all three levels, assuming, for example, that the Bible provided important literal "data" about Jesus's life and work. But he was more interested in the higher levels of meaning—what the Scripture said about living a godly life and how the soul can be drawn to the presence God.

- Origen looked for symbolic meaning throughout the Bible. He noted, for example, that in Revelation 19, Christ is identified as the Word, or in Greek, *logos*. Logos can refer to a simple spoken word, but it also has the sense of divine thought or reason. Origen thus interprets the tangible, earthly form of Jesus as God's logos, which has the power to open up the heavens and give people a deeper knowledge of God.

- Further, Origen believed that the cosmic battle in Revelation 19 takes place in the human soul and that the seven-headed beast symbolizes the destructive forces at work within the individual. The logos—divine reason—does battle with the irrational forces and impulses that seek to dominate people from within. The battle of Armageddon is an ongoing struggle that is waged wherever God's Word fights against the power of untruth.

- This kind of spiritual reading set a major direction for interpreting Revelation in the generations that followed, and over time, the interpretations of the symbolism in Revelation became more and more elaborate.

- It's interesting that Origen sees the forces of the beast at work in people, including himself. We have a tendency to think that the beast always symbolizes something that is "out there," but Origen notes that the forces of deception operate in all of us.

Internal Repetitions

- The 3rd-century Christian Victorinus wrote the earliest known sustained commentary on Revelation. His great insight, which still has an impact on scholarship today, was that the plot of Revelation doesn't unfold in a straight line. Instead, the book repeats the same basic message multiple times in multiple forms.

- As we've seen, many have read Revelation as a linear account of world history, leading up to the end of the age. But by highlighting the phenomenon of internal repetition, Victorinus shows us that the Apocalypse can't easily be turned into a step-by-step outline of coming events.

- Victorinus noted, for example, that the middle of Revelation describes a series of plagues that occur when the seven angels blow their trumpets. A few chapters later, the angels pour out seven bowls, and the same plagues are visited on the earth. For Victorinus, these plagues were symbolic warnings of coming persecution.

- The insistence of Victorinus that the author repeated these symbols to make a point was an important insight. Revelation was not predicting a chronological series of two sets of plagues but using multiple sets of images to make the same theological point.

- Some decades after the death of Victorinus, his work was picked up by Jerome, the scholar who produced the Latin translation of the Bible used in the Western church for centuries. Jerome revised Victorinus's commentary on the millennium, which he found too worldly. For Jerome, the millennial kingdom is a symbol for a godly way of life. It exists wherever people live lives of obedience and chastity.

Revelation's Sense of Time

- Tyconius was a Latin-speaking North African who lived in the 4th century; Augustine, also a North African, lived into the early 5th. Tyconius belonged to a Christian group known as the Donatists, while Augustine was a Catholic. These groups sharply disagreed about some church matters, but both Tyconius and Augustine agreed that Christians were already living in the millennial age.

- Tyconius and Augustine identified the binding of Satan in Revelation as the First Coming of Christ, which had occurred several centuries before their time. They noted that in the gospels, when Jesus performed an exorcism, he said that he was binding Satan, whom he compared to a strong man. For these thinkers, then, Jesus's ministry on earth was when the millennium began.

- As these writers developed this basic idea, they also spiritualized it. They argued that the image of Satan being bound in the abyss was to be understood symbolically as the way in which Satan was bound in the abyss of human hearts. This allowed them to say that the power of evil was still at work in the world, through the destructive actions of human beings, yet it was also true that evil was not allowed to operate freely.

- For Tyconius and Augustine, the resurrection of the faithful was also symbolic. The first resurrection occurs when people are raised up to the new life of Christian faith at the time of baptism. The second resurrection is the one that Christians can expect to occur in the future, just before the last judgment. The second resurrection is what Paul referred to as the resurrection of the body, a transformed existence into endless life.

- It is intriguing to ask where the Antichrist fits into this picture, given that many early Christians expected the Antichrist to persecute the church at the end of the age. Augustine noted that the New Testament of First John said that it was already the last hour and that many antichrists had come. These were the people who denied the humanity of Christ by refusing to show love for others.

- Toward the end of *The City of God*, Augustine affirmed that the millennial age would someday come to an end. But he also thought that the period of 1,000 years was symbolic, so there is no way of knowing when the end would come.

Suggested Reading

Daley, "Apocalypticism in Early Christian Theology."

Fredriksen, "Tyconius and Augustine on the Apocalypse."

Questions to Consider

1. Revelation's visions of conflict originally included a sharp critique of Roman imperialism. Through spiritual interpretation, these visions were applied to the conflict with evil that occurs within each person and within the church. What might be gained by such spiritual reading? What might be lost by such spiritual reading?

2. Victorinus maintained that Revelation repeats the same basic message several times through various images. How might interpreters who adopt this approach read Revelation differently from those who expect the book to map out a linear series of events?

The Key to the Meaning of History
Lecture 16

I n the past few lectures, we've encountered some ancient approaches to the interpretation of Revelation that may seem peculiar to modern readers. Yet when we reflect on the questions those ancient writers sought to answer, we often find that we are asking similar questions. In this lecture, we'll consider the interpretations of ancient writers who sought to explore the meaning of history and their own place within it. As modern readers, we, too, want a sense of where things have been and where they are going so that we can navigate our way through life. The ancient writers that we will consider were trying to make sense of history from a theological point of view, to interpret the flow of events in light of the purposes of God. To gain a deeper understanding of this approach, we will look at some of these writers at three moments in time, ranging from late antiquity to the High Middle Ages.

Late Antiquity: A Time of Triumph

- A major event that occurred for Christians in late antiquity was the change in the church's relationship to the Roman Empire that occurred under Constantine. When the emperor Constantine and his successors embraced the Christian faith, the church moved from its earlier, more tenuous position to become the dominant religion of the empire.

- Tracing this shift is particularly interesting for our focus on the Apocalypse, the most anti-imperial book in the New Testament. How would the author of Revelation have reacted to the idea that the Roman emperors now claimed Jesus as their own? Would he have been horrified by the phenomenon of a Christian empire, or would he have seen it as the triumph of God?

Constantine's triumphal arch is one of the most impressive monuments in Rome.

- As we saw in the last lecture, Tyconius and Augustine concluded that the church was already in the millennial age and that people entered this spiritual kingdom through baptism. But they also recognized that spiritual conflict was ongoing and that God needed to keep the forces of evil in check through his work among the faithful.

- It's important to note that Tyconius and Augustine did not have a progressive view of history. They did not think that things would gradually improve. They believed that the spiritual struggle would continue in its present form until God defeated evil at the end of the age. They also refrained from equating the visible structures of the empire with those of the kingdom of God.

- Others in this period were more ready to celebrate the formation of a Christian empire, as can be seen in Christian art and architecture from the 5th century onward. Some of the motifs in the artwork from this period are taken from the heavenly throne room scenes of Revelation, and the form of the Roman emperors' triumphal arch was integrated into the architecture of Roman churches.

The Middle Ages: A Time of Threat

- In the 7th, 8th, and 9th centuries, the seemingly victorious Christian empire had become fragmented. Some of the eastern regions were now part of the Byzantine Empire, which was centered at Constantinople. Other parts of the east and all of North Africa were part of the Islamic Empire, and in the west were the Latin-speaking Christians.

- The unity of the west collapsed in the 10th century, leaving various warlords to pursue their own interests without any effective control by the state. The west was also plagued by external threats—the Vikings from the north, the Magyars from the east, and Muslim forces from the south.

- During the mid-10th century, a French abbot named Adso wrote a treatise called "The Origin and Time of the Antichrist," in which he recast a number of earlier apocalyptic traditions in an effort to help people understand the direction of history. His work included words of both warning and encouragement.

- The bad news Adso announced was that people could expect a final outpouring of evil when the Antichrist was unleashed. Adso painted a picture of the Antichrist as the consummate villain, who would enter the rebuilt temple and proclaim himself as God. He would then assume his role as the beast and persecute the church, but he was ultimately doomed to be killed on the Mount of Olives in Jerusalem.

- The good news was that a hero called the last world emperor would arise from the midst of the people and revitalize the Christian empire. The legend of the last world emperor was a way of affirming that the Latin kingdom and its rulers had a positive role to play in God's plan. Adso assured people that as long as the empire continued, the Antichrist would not be unleashed.

- By the time of the Middle Ages, Revelation's battle of good versus evil had undergone a transformation. The beast no longer signified the Roman Empire but was a tyrant who threatened what had become the Christian Roman Empire. Adso's story called people to value the structures of government that kept chaos at bay and encouraged them to maintain their commitment to their leadership.

The High Middle Ages: A Time of Reform
- By the 11th and 12th centuries, the threats of tribal invasions were essentially over. The Holy Roman Empire provided a sense of stability and the Latin church held a commanding position in European society. At the same time, there was also mismanagement in government and scandal among the clergy, prompting calls for serious reform.

- The most notable reformer was Pope Gregory VII, who worked to ensure that the church was not subordinate to the empire. His ideal was that priests would ultimately oversee kings and princes, as well as the people, and the clergy would be raised to new heights of moral and spiritual life.

- Another reformer was the 12th-century figure Joachim of Fiore. He had traveled to the Holy Land and had a spiritual experience that caused him to devote himself to the religious life. He ultimately founded his own monastery and came to view himself as an inspired interpreter of the Bible, especially the book of Revelation.

- Through a mystical illumination, Joachim arrived at the idea that the entire flow of history mirrored the character of God. Because God is a Trinity—Father, Son, and Holy Spirit—history itself must be a trinity. Thus, Joachim pictured time as divided into three circles, like links on a chain.

- The first circle in Joachim's visualization represented the period of God the Father, which mainly corresponded to the Old Testament. The second circle was the period of God the Son, which was essentially from the New Testament down to Joachim's own time. The third circle was the period of God the Holy Spirit, which Joachim expected to be a new spiritual age that had been inaugurated and would fully emerge in the future.

- Recall that for Augustine, history was not a progressive movement into a new age, but for Joachim, it was. That is why he called for reform and renewed spiritual discipline: Given that time itself was moving toward the spiritual age, people must conform to spiritual ideas in order to conform to the flow of history.

- Along with this progressive view of history, Joachim had a profound sense that the turn of the ages would involve an intensified struggle with evil. Within each of his three main periods of history, he envisioned seven threats to the church, akin to the seven heads of the dragon in Revelation. According to Joachim's conception, the seventh threat—the Antichrist himself—would soon arrive.

- This interpretation gave Joachim and many of his readers a way to find meaning in what might otherwise seem to be a pointless struggle against evils that beset the church in every period of its existence. By including a symbolic outline of history in the images of Revelation, Joachim found assurance that God was ultimately guiding the course of events to its proper conclusion.

Suggested Reading

McGinn, *Apocalyptic Spirituality*, pp. 81–148.

Reeves, *Joachim of Fiore and the Prophetic Future*, chapter 1.

1. Revelation was composed in the 1st century, and its author was highly critical of imperial Rome. Beginning in the 4th century, the empire was ruled by Christian emperors, and images from Revelation were thought to support the Christian empire's role in protecting the faith and social order. How might differences in social and political context affect the way modern readers understand Revelation?

2. Spiritual interpretation of Revelation focused on God's relationship to individuals and the church. Joachim used Revelation to develop an entire theory of history. Why might some people have become dissatisfied with the older spiritual approach? Why might the newer historical approach have had such appeal?

Apocalyptic Fervor in the Late Middle Ages
Lecture 17

In the last lecture, we saw how the question of the meaning of history led Joachim of Fiore to search for a way to conceive of time as a whole, and in this task, he made wide use of the Apocalypse. In this lecture, we will see that this way of thinking caused people to view themselves as participants in an ongoing apocalyptic drama. It was a way of reading Revelation that differed from the older spiritual interpretations, which had focused on the internal struggles of the individual. In the Middle Ages, we'll see Revelation turned into a map of history, a reading that had explosive potential.

Joachim's Legacy

- As mentioned in the last lecture, Joachim thought that the seven heads of the great dragon in Revelation pointed to seven periods in the history of the church, extending from Jesus and the early church into the late 12th century. Joachim also believed that other visions in Revelation covered this same period of time.

- The visions of the seven seals were particularly important for Joachim because he assumed that each one symbolized a successive period of time. For example, the first seal, which unleashed the conquering horseman, symbolized the triumphant founding of the church by Christ and the apostles in the 1st century. Joachim believed that his own time was on the verge of the sixth seal.

- According to Revelation, the sixth seal would be a time of cosmic upheaval, when the sun would become black and the moon would turn to blood. For Joachim, this cosmic upheaval was equated with social upheaval that would occur at the end of the present age and would include the persecution of the righteous by forces opposed to reform.

- This chronological reading of the seals also carried a hopeful message. According to Revelation, in the time of the sixth seal, an angel would ascend from the rising of the sun, bearing the seal of the living God. Joachim thought this angel symbolized a specific individual, perhaps a pope, who would arise to renew the Christian faith and preach the word of God.

- The distress experienced under the sixth seal would lead to the opening of the seventh seal, which in Revelation, brought a period of graceful silence. For Joachim, this silence was a symbol of the Sabbath rest that awaited the world at the consummation of this epoch of history.

Calculating the End of the Age

- Joachim and those who followed him believed that they were living in a period that began with Jesus and included the whole subsequent history of the church. How much longer, they wondered, would the period of Jesus last?

- According to Joachim, the answer, derived from the Gospel of Matthew, was 42 generations, or 1260 years. Interestingly, the number 1260 appears in Revelation as the number of days God's two witnesses would prophesy and the time that the woman who represented the faithful found refuge in the wilderness.

- Joachim made another point that would have dramatic consequences for the generations that followed. He believed that the two witnesses in Revelation 11 symbolized two monastic orders that would use prayer and preaching to resist the forces of the Antichrist. Shortly after Joachim died, two new monastic leaders did appear: Saint Dominic and Saint Francis.

The Dominicans and the Franciscans

- Both Dominic and Francis founded monastic orders devoted to an austere lifestyle. Although neither of these men seemed to have much interest in the apocalyptic dimension of history, an apocalyptic worldview became influential among some of their followers in the 13th century. Both groups adopted the idea that their orders would fulfill biblical prophecy and play a key role in the final stage of history.

- Both groups also adopted Joachim's idea that time had advanced through the first six seals of Revelation. They believed that the time of social upheaval equated with the cosmic upheaval in Revelation was underway. Further, the Franciscans believed that the angel in Revelation bearing the seal of God was Francis himself, who had received the stigmata.

- Many of those who followed the direction that Joachim had set came to see themselves as players in an apocalyptic drama. They were the ones who bore witness to the truth, even when they encountered resistance; thus, their role had a legitimate place in God's plan.

A Split in the Franciscan Order

- A scandal was created in the Franciscan order by a young member who wrote a book called *An Introduction to the Eternal Gospel.* The expression "eternal gospel" recalls a vision in Revelation 14, in which an angel with an "eternal gospel" announces that the time of judgment has arrived. According to the young Franciscan, the eternal gospel had been brought to the world by Joachim of Fiore.

- Further, this young Franciscan author announced that the present-age church would end in the year 1260 and that, in the new age, the writings of Joachim would replace both the Old and New Testaments.

- The year 1260 came and went without incident, but apocalyptic intensity continued and helped to split the Franciscan order into two groups: a radical group (the "Spirituals") that insisted on a life of absolute poverty and a more moderate group. The moderate group believed it was acceptable to partake of the worldly goods of the papal establishment as long as the Franciscans did not own them.

- One of the Franciscans who used Revelation to legitimate the stance of the Spirituals on the matter of poverty was Peter John Olivi. Olivi expected the Antichrist to come in stages that would include a false pope attacking the ideal of poverty. Not long after this, a new pope assumed office and began fulfilling the apocalyptic role that Olivi had laid out for him.

Dover Pictorial Archive.

Founder of the Franciscan order, Saint Francis was so spiritually intense that he was said to have had a vision in which he received the five wounds of Christ on his own body.

- This pope sided with the moderates and worked to suppress the radical Franciscans. Of course, from the radicals' perspective, this was persecution—exactly what was expected of the Antichrist. They had all the more reason to resist in order to fulfill their own apocalyptic calling as witnesses to the truth.

- The conflict continued, and a succeeding pope condemned outright the Franciscan ideal of poverty. For the radicals, this meant that Olivi's prophecy had been fulfilled: If the ideal of poverty was integral to following Christ, the pope's denial of the ideal meant that he was the Antichrist.

- The process of turning Revelation into a "script" that lays out the final events of history invites people to see themselves as players in a great apocalyptic drama. Further, this perspective encourages tenacious resistance and the tendency to demonize the opponents. In this situation, compromise is impossible.

Medieval Politics
- This drama was not limited to the internal affairs of the church. It also shaped a major power struggle between the church and the state or, more precisely, between the pope and the emperor. The emperor in this case was Frederick II, one of the great Antichrist figures in world history. Frederick was ambitious, did not seem particularly devout, and had no inclination to respect the usual boundaries of the papal territory.

- When Frederick failed to carry out a new Crusade to the Holy Land, the pope put the emperor under a declaration of excommunication. Later, when Frederick made moves to solidify his control over northern Italy, he was excommunicated a second time. As the conflict progressed, Frederick besieged some towns and cities, ruined others, and gave orders to sink or capture the ships that brought church leaders to Rome.

- Not surprisingly, the conflict took on apocalyptic dimensions. Pope Gregory IX issued a letter that attacked the emperor as the blasphemous beast that rises out of the sea from Revelation 13. The emperor's own propaganda machine responded that the pope was the great red dragon of Revelation 12.

- The conflict continued under Gregory's successor, Pope Innocent IV. Because Frederick's power was so strong in Italy, the pope was forced to flee to southern France, where he launched a campaign to depose the emperor. Even after Frederick's death, his allies tried to equate the pope with the Antichrist, while on the papal side, Frederick became, like Nero, a monstrous tyrant who had purportedly died yet proved to be alive.

- This series of events exemplifies the results of attempting to turn Revelation into a map of the end of history. Such a perspective invites people to see themselves as key players in the drama and to make direct connections between Revelation's vision of the beast and individual leaders.

- As we have seen, however, the visions in Revelation did not predict a series of specific events that would take place in the ordinary realm of time and space. The images of horsemen, beasts, and dragons unfold in a kaleidoscopic way that persistently defies human attempts to reduce them to a timeline.

Suggested Reading

McGinn, "Apocalypticism and Church Reform."

Potestà, "Radical Apocalyptic Movements in the Late Middle Ages."

Questions to Consider

1. In the late Middle Ages, it became increasingly common to charge that one's political or religious opponent was the Antichrist and the beast of Revelation. This polemical use of apocalyptic language might be effective in some social contexts but not in others. What would be required for a term like "Antichrist" to sway public perceptions of a leader?

2. In the late Middle Ages, the book of Revelation became especially popular in religious groups that stood outside the dominant church structures. Why might this have been the case? Would a similar pattern also be true today? Why or why not?

Luther, Radicals, and Roman Catholics
Lecture 18

In this lecture, we move from the late Middle Ages into the 16th century and the world of the Reformation. This period includes a fascinating group of characters: Martin Luther, a renegade monk; Thomas Müntzer, the architect of a failed political revolution; and Melchior Hoffmann, an apocalyptic prophet who thought that his own career had been foretold in Revelation. To round out this cast, we'll also meet some Catholic thinkers who responded to the apocalyptic rhetoric of the time by redefining the way people saw the book of Revelation itself.

Luther's First Preface to Revelation

- As many of us know, Martin Luther was the monk and teacher who posted his 95 theses on the church door at Wittenberg, protesting abuses in the Catholic Church. He later spent time at a castle called the Wartburg in a kind of exile from church life.

- While at the Wartburg, Luther began compiling a translation of the New Testament into German, complete with prefaces to each of the biblical books. In his preface to Revelation, he denied that the book was apostolic because it did not speak clearly about Christ. As Luther wrote, "Christ is neither taught nor known in it."

- For Luther, Christ was the center of the Scriptures, meaning that the Bible's message centered on the actions of God to restore his relationship with human beings through the death and resurrection of Jesus. Because Revelation did not speak clearly about what God had done in Christ on behalf of the world, the book had little value in Luther's eyes.

- Luther also pointed out that Revelation was filled with visions and images that simply confused people. He insisted that if a true apostolic writing is supposed to give people a clear and accessible message about Christ, then Revelation fell abysmally short.

- Luther may have seemed dismissive of Revelation in what he wrote in his preface, but Revelation was the only book in his German New Testament that was illustrated from start to finish. The illustrations offered a highly polemical critique of the papacy, which Luther had come to think of as the Antichrist.

- Luther insisted that his work was bringing new clarity to the message of Christ. But papal authorities had condemned what Luther taught, which meant that they were speaking against his emphasis on Christ and were, thus, anti-Christ.

- From Luther's perspective, the whole series of past popes had elevated themselves above the Word of God. They claimed authority to govern affairs on earth; extorted money from Germany for extravagant projects in Rome; and used heavy-handed tactics to suppress reform. For Luther, these actions made the papal office itself the seat of the Antichrist.

- In the illustrations that accompanied Luther's translation of Revelation (done by Lucas Cranach in the style of Albrecht Dürer), the beast and the harlot wear the papal headgear. Clearly, the papacy was riding on the beastly power of the Antichrist and had made the world into a harlot's kingdom.

Luther's Second Preface to Revelation

- Luther's 1522 preface to Revelation took a negative stance against the book's confusing visions, while the illustrations used in his translation furthered his conflict with the papacy. As the decade progressed, Luther saw some positive results from his efforts at reform, but disagreements over matters of doctrine and practice continued.

- In 1530, Luther wrote a second preface to Revelation that offers a chapter-by-chapter discussion of the book. This preface reverts to the late-medieval practice of turning Revelation into a map of history.

- On one level, the 1530 preface seems like just one more fanciful futuristic interpretation. But at the end, Luther drops the historical decoding and asks a breathtakingly simple question: How can Revelation actually be helpful to the reader?

- Luther's answer is that Revelation warns us against thinking that anyone can see the kingdom of God on earth. The book is brutally honest about the shortcomings and conflicts that exist in the church and society, and if you're looking for the kingdom, the seemingly endless problems may drive you to despair. But despite all the conflict, people are not alone; Christ remains active in the world.

- Having dismissed Revelation, then attempting to decode it, then turning it into a polemic against his opponents, Luther finally arrives at a theological stance: Revelation is best read as a message that calls for realism about the shortcomings of each generation but ultimate hope for the future.

The Radical Wing of the Reformation

- Where Luther read Revelation in light of his understanding of Christ, other figures in his time read it in light of their claims to have received direct revelations from God. One of these figures was Thomas Müntzer, who insisted that he had received insights directly from God that went beyond Scripture. Müntzer believed that the last judgment was fast approaching and that he was going to play a role in it.

- Müntzer saw the power of the Antichrist at work in the whole religious and social hierarchy of the late-medieval world. In his eyes, the papacy shared in the work of the Antichrist by supporting the status quo, but for Müntzer, it was the whole structure of society that was anti-Christ.

- He concluded that the coming kingdom of God meant that political power was to be transferred from the feudal authorities to the common people. He expected this to occur though an apocalyptic battle in which he would play a part.

- In 1524–25, a group of German peasants rose up against their landlords, and Müntzer urged them on. As the revolt spread, Müntzer became a local leader, but his career ended when the revolt was ruthlessly put down and Müntzer himself was executed.

- Not all of the radical reformers advocated violent overthrow of the government. A good example of the alternative was Melchior Hoffmann, who emerged in the 1520s as a fiery lay preacher and an advocate of Luther's reforms. Hoffman came to believe that he had received special revelations from God, and his unorthodox message forced him to move to Sweden, then Strasbourg.

After initially dismissing the book of Revelation, Luther decoded it and came up with a theological insight that completely overturned what he had said before.

- In Strasbourg, he found several kindred spirits, who also claimed to have the gift of prophecy. On the basis of the visions they received, Hoffmann became convinced that he was one of the two witnesses described in Revelation 11. Further, the city of Strasbourg would be the spiritual Jerusalem, where Christ would set up his kingdom. The events leading up to the kingdom would occur by 1533.

- In 1533, Hoffman was arrested by the authorities at Strasbourg. As one of God's witnesses, he knew that he must be condemned by the agents of the beast before the end of the age could come. But history refused to cooperate. The apocalyptic year passed without incident, and Hoffmann languished in prison for 10 years before his death.

The Contributions of the Jesuits

- . The most important Catholic contributions to the dialogue about reform and Revelation were made by the Jesuits later in the 16th century. Their approach was to create distance between the message of Revelation and the papacy. Some did this by saying that Revelation's message pertained mainly to the future, and others said it pertained mainly to the past, but either way, it had nothing to do with the present pope.

- One of the scholars who pushed the message of Revelation into the future was the Jesuit Robert Bellarmine. He responded to the Protestants by going back to the biblical texts on which the Antichrist tradition was built and pointing out that they did not apply to the popes, either past or present. Thus, the whole business about the Antichrist belonged somewhere off in the future.

- This perspective was applied systematically to Revelation by another Jesuit, Francisco Ribera. He rejected the idea that Revelation mapped out the epochs of history, claiming that the book had to do with things that were still to come.

- Another Jesuit, Luis Alcazar, achieved a similar result by pushing the message of Revelation back in time. He said that the book addressed the situation of the church under the pagan Roman emperors, not the Christian popes. Thus, all of its visions—except those at the very end—must have been realized before the empire became Christian.

- These efforts to distance Revelation from the present meant that the book came to have a more marginal role in the Catholic tradition, with the exception of providing much of the standard imagery for the Virgin Mary. The sense of radiance used to describe the mother of the Messiah in Revelation 12 fit well with the Catholic conception of Mary's purity from the taint of original sin.

Krey, "Luther and the Apocalypse."

Petersen, *Preaching in the Last Days*, chap. 4.

Questions to Consider

1. Martin Luther dealt with Revelation in at least three different ways: First, he dismissed the book as having no value. Second, he tried to decode the book by relating it to events throughout history. Third, he concluded with a theological interpretation that warned of the church's failings and called for hope in the victory of Christ. What problems and possibilities arise from each of these three options?

2. Roman Catholic interpreters in this period also dealt with Revelation in at least three ways: First, some argued that most of Revelation pertained to the distant past, near the time when the book was written. Second, others argued that most of Revelation pertained to the distant future. Third, some selectively used imagery from Revelation for artistic and devotional purposes, as in the portrayal of Mary. What problems and possibilities arise from each of these three options?

Revelation Takes Musical Form
Lecture 19

In the two lectures, we have seen the book of Revelation play a turbulent role in the late-medieval power struggles among popes, emperors, and church reformers. The polemical use of Revelation continued to be all too common in the years that followed the Protestant Reformation. In this lecture, however, we will consider Revelation from a completely different perspective, a musical one. As we will see, Revelation is one of the most musical books in the Bible; it incorporates many songs and has inspired countless more. The polemics fade when we look at Revelation musically, and what remains is a vivid sense of joy, hope, and fellowship.

The Songs of Revelation

- Music is built into the structure of the book of Revelation itself. Revelation includes a number of major cycles of visions, and each cycle ends with a song of praise.

- For example, the first major section of Revelation consists of the messages to the seven churches, followed by the vision of the heavenly throne room. There, we find a group of mysterious creatures who raise their voices to proclaim the worthiness of God. Songs are also sung after the visions of the seven seals and the seven trumpets.

- These songs of praise from Revelation were later used by musicians in their own compositions. By allowing worshipers to sing the songs of Revelation, composers enabled them to become participants in John's celestial scenes. The effect was to create a community in which people felt more deeply connected to God and to one another.

The Lutheran Tradition

- The idea of putting images from Revelation into music was not new, but it gained a special kind of energy as a result of the Protestant Reformation. Luther and the reformers had given renewed emphasis to the reading and preaching of Scripture in their communities. They also gave a prominent place to the singing of hymns, which became one of the hallmarks of worship for Lutherans and many other Protestants.

- Of course, if we look at the music that grew out of the Lutheran tradition, it does not take us long to get to Johann Sebastian Bach, whose music was deeply informed by his Lutheran faith. The composition that we will consider is "Wake, Awake, for Night Is Flying."

- This piece began as a popular Lutheran hymn, originally written by a man named Philipp Nicolai. The song begins with images from the Hebrew prophets. As the first verse is sung, the darkness of night is fading, and the watchmen of the city are calling out to announce the arrival of the new day.

- After the first verse, the words of the hymn are taken from Jesus's parable of the wedding banquet. In the Bible, Jesus told of wedding guests waiting during the night for the bridegroom to come so that the wedding festival could begin. When the groom arrived, the guests would light their lamps to welcome him.

- In the last verse of the hymn, images inspired by the last chapters of Revelation appear. In this verse, Nicolai sought to duplicate the sense of hope conveyed by Revelation's description of the gates of New Jerusalem and the glory that would be experienced by those who entered. In doing so, he draws everyone who sings this hymn into the presence of God.

- This hymn originated as a militant statement of joy in the face of what seemed like unending grief. It was written at a time when a devastating plague was sweeping through Germany. Nicolai, a pastor, wanted people to picture themselves as waiting for the dawn of a new day that was sure to come, waiting for the night of despair to end with the radiant brightness of God's city.

The Music of Handel

- One of Bach's contemporaries was George Frideric Handel. Handel was also of German background, but he spent much of his career in London and wrote much of his music for the theater.

- Handel also wrote oratorios focused on religious themes, the most famous of which is the *Messiah*. The script for this piece was compiled by a man named Charles Jennens from various parts of the Bible. The words of the Hallelujah Chorus are a musical rendering of lines drawn from two passages in Revelation 19 and one in Revelation 11.

Handel blended the sacred and the secular, and he was quite willing to take a spiritual message into a secular space.

- The *Messiah* was written during the Enlightenment, a time when reason and rationalism were valued. In the realm of religion, it seemed reasonable to keep a place for the idea of God and to retain a traditional sense of moral behavior. But when rationalism was taken to an extreme, it elevated the life of the mind in ways that neglected the needs of the spirit. This is where works like the *Messiah* played a role.

- On one level, Handel's *Messiah* is a thoughtful and reasonable work; the piece arranges passages from the Bible in a clear sequence, illustrating the coherence of the biblical message. But the rising of the music in the Hallelujah Chorus takes people into a realm beyond reason and rationality and into the mystery of divine joy.

The Songwriter Charles Wesley

- The Englishman Charles Wesley was a younger contemporary of Bach and Handel and a prolific songwriter. During his time at Oxford, he and his brother formed a group dedicated to personal spiritual discipline. Eventually, this group became known as the Methodists.

- When Wesley and others issued a call for spiritual renewal in the Church of England, many of the established churches closed their doors to Methodist preachers. Thus, the Wesley brothers decided to take their preaching to the streets and fields. As their movement grew, opposition to the Methodists became intense and, sometimes, violent.

- Wesley chose to respond to this opposition by compiling a collection of songs: *Hymns for Times of Trouble and Persecution*. The words of these hymns were designed to lift the spirits of those who found themselves demoralized by conflict. Within this collection were several songs meant to be, as Wesley said, "sung in a tumult."

- Probably the best known song from this collection is entitled "Ye Servants of God, Your Master Proclaim," at the end of which are words drawn from Revelation. The song moves from conflict into joy, ending with exuberant words of thanks and celebration from the Apocalypse. It's striking that the songs that were sung in Revelation took on new life when sung in the street.

Revelation in American Gospel Music

- The traditional American hymn "Shall We Gather at the River?" actually originated not in a rural context but in Brooklyn, New York. The songwriter was Robert Lowry, a Baptist pastor during the Civil War.

- By the year 1864, the war had taken a tremendous toll on American life and morale, and Brooklyn was experiencing a long, hot summer. According to Lowry, as he lay down to rest one day in a state of near exhaustion, he thought of Revelation's New Jerusalem, with the throne of God and the river of life that flowed from it. For Lowry, that was the scene that pointed to the time beyond death, where those who had lost their loved ones had the hope of a reunion in God's endless day.

- As Lowry thought of that scene, he was struck by how much attention was given to the presence of mortality, to what he called the "river of death." He wanted to offset that emphasis by inviting people to participate in the hope that was signified by the river of life.

- The songs we've mentioned in this lecture are just a small sample of the pieces that have been inspired by Revelation. Today, Christian communities embody both traditional and contemporary styles of worship, and often, the worshipers are unaware that they are singing words from Revelation, words that shape the way they think about God, themselves, and the community to which they belong.

Suggested Reading

Stapert, *Handel's Messiah*.

Tyson, *Assist Me to Proclaim*, especially chap. 8.

1. Musicians have often drawn images from the festive and hopeful scenes that occur at major turning points in Revelation. Do the composers noted in this lecture make appropriate use of the language and imagery of Revelation? Why or why not?

2. How might the musical compositions based on Revelation enhance a reader's appreciation of Revelation itself? How might familiarity with Revelation enhance one's appreciation of the musical compositions?

Revelation in African American Culture
Lecture 20

In the last lecture, we saw how images from Revelation took musical form in Europe and North America. We will continue our musical exploration in this lecture, but we will focus more specifically on African American culture. As we've seen, music has given the language and imagery of Revelation some of its most enduring forms, and the reverse is also true. As we look at the songs the Apocalypse has inspired, we may discover possibilities in the book that we might never have discerned otherwise. Musicians, certainly those in the African American tradition, have proven to be some of the book's most creative and engaging interpreters.

"I Have a Dream"

- In his famous "I Have a Dream" speech, Martin Luther King Jr., wove together biblical themes to make a ringing call for social justice in America. At the end of the speech, he referred to "the old spiritual," and the theme of the spiritual he quoted is freedom.

National Archives (306-SSM-4D-107-8).

Martin Luther King Jr. envisioned the day when all people would sing the words of the old spiritual, "Thank God Almighty, we are free at last!"

- The specific words that King quoted don't come from Revelation, but many spirituals do use themes from this book. Such spirituals often allude to the singer's hope for deliverance, freedom, and a better life in the presence of God. These songs reinforce the sense that the future is ultimately open, which in turn, fosters a willingness to resist being held captive by the present.

- Some have assumed that the emphasis on heavenly imagery in spirituals was originally a way to foster acceptance of the status quo among African American slaves. But that perspective has been challenged by those who have seen that hope for the future can foster spiritual resistance and social change in the present.

Sojourner Truth

- Sojourner Truth was one of the most famous African American women of the 19th century. She was active in the campaigns for women's rights and the abolition of slavery. She was also a lay preacher, whose favorite hymn centered on Revelation's New Jerusalem.

- Born a slave in New York State around 1797, when she was about 30, Sojourner Truth had a spiritual experience in which she sensed the presence of Jesus. This eventually led her to a gathering of local Methodists, where she heard a hymn that pointedly described two contrasting realities: the vision of God's city and the reality of human suffering.

Sojourner Truth's favorite hymn centered on Revelation's New Jerusalem.

- The hymn begins with some classic images from Revelation: a light-filled city, a temple, and saints in white robes. But then it speaks of the afflictions and trials of the singers. The hymn recognizes that if affliction is the reality that defines a person's future, then the natural response is despair. It counters that despair with images from Revelation that open up a different future, offering the singers incentive to persevere in the present.

- As mentioned earlier, some have wondered whether these hopeful images lead people to acceptance of the status quo. That was certainly not the case for Sojourner Truth. She became the first African American woman to win a case against a white man in court and dedicated her life to a career of social reform.

African American Musical Forms
- The spiritual was closely connected to the slave communities of the American South. Spirituals were created orally, and this quality makes them challenging to study, because the lyrics and melodies evolved as the songs passed from one group of singers to another.

- One such song, called "There's a Meeting Here Tonight," explicitly tells us that its text comes from Matthew and Revelation. Some have noted that the images and ideas of the Apocalypse may have resonated particularly with slaves because West African traditions placed a great deal of emphasis on the spirit.

- Another aspect of Revelation that was appealing was the ease with which it moved from the earthly world to the heavenly one and from the present age into the future. For the slaves, that ease of movement was freeing.

Freedom in This World and the Next
- As we know, the New Jerusalem vision is the climax of the book of Revelation. Evil, suffering, and death have been eliminated, and people are invited into the radiant presence of God. One of the spirituals that draws on this scene is "Blow Your Trumpet, Gabriel."

- The singer here calls on Gabriel to "blow me home to the New Jerusalem," which on one level, seems otherworldly. According to Revelation, people will enter the city after they have died and been resurrected.

- However, death doesn't seem to be the issue in this song. Instead, the singer wants Gabriel to change things for the better with a blast of his horn. He wants to be whisked away from life in the present to a place called "home." Thus, New Jerusalem becomes the place one feels at home, and we get the sense that the singer might get a taste of it in the present if he came to a place where he felt he truly belonged.

- The tree of life is also featured in this song, which again, might lead us to think that the singer is speaking about the next world. But in the world of spirituals, the tree of life easily became a metaphor for the opportunities that made for a better life, wherever that was to be found—in this world or the next.

- The slaves who sang these spirituals were confined by a social system from which many saw little chance of escape. Yet the songs pressed the imagination beyond the confines of the present, evoking scenes of a different future. Even in the context of social and legal bondage, the music and its apocalyptic imagery fostered a sense of spiritual freedom.

"My Father, How Long?"
- The spiritual called "My Father, How Long?" had been sung for many years in slave communities, but at the beginning of the American Civil War, one could be jailed for singing it. It was viewed as subversive because its otherworldly imagery too easily lent itself to supporting the quest for freedom in this world.

- The song starts off by asking how long "this poor sinner" will suffer on earth, and the refrain answers that it won't be long. The singer will soon be called home by the Lord to walk the golden streets of New Jerusalem.

- But the song also includes the words "we will soon be free," which seem to blur the line between the future and the present. If New Jerusalem is equivalent to freedom, then people might look for a taste of it wherever freedom is created.

Gospel in the Urban North

- The New Jerusalem theme also played a role in the late 19th and early 20th centuries among African Americans who had moved north after the war. One of the musical traditions that developed at that time was what we think of as the gospel sound, with its tight harmonies and sense of driving rhythm.

- The old lyrics about the city of God took on a new vitality for people who were actually living in major cities. And when urban life fell short of the vision of Revelation, the music helped keep a sense of hope alive.

- One of the older spirituals that became a popular gospel number was called "Oh, What a Beautiful City." This song describes gates on every side of the city, beckoning people into the reality of life in New Jerusalem. Clearly, this promise of access overturns the sense of exclusion that was common in many earthly cities and could inspire efforts to bring about greater freedom and dignity for those who suffered it.

Dixieland Jazz and the Theme of Cosmic Judgment

- The African American tradition sometimes weaves together images of cosmic judgment with images of hope. For us, it's interesting to ask whether the prospect of cosmic judgment is good news or bad news, and the surprising answer in some African American music is: It depends.

- For those who are doing well in the present, the prospect of cosmic change will inevitably seem bad. But for those who are oppressed, shaking things up creates the possibility of a better life. Probably the most influential rendition of this perspective comes to us in the form of Dixieland jazz.

- This form of music was developed by African American musicians in the late 19th and early 20th centuries. Perhaps the most famous Dixieland song, "When the Saints Go Marching In," originated as a musical rendition of the Apocalypse.

- This song connects cosmic images of judgment from Revelation 6—the darkening of the sun and the moon's transformation to blood—with the vision of the saints in glory from Revelation 7. The reference to being in "that number" recalls the great multitude that John saw, the crowd that finds life with God.

Suggested Reading

Blount, *Can I Get a Witness?*

Mabee, *Sojourner Truth.*

Questions to Consider

1. Images of New Jerusalem had an important place in African American music. How might such images have encouraged a sense of acceptance of current conditions? How might such images have encouraged active efforts for social change, as in the case of Sojourner Truth?

2. The hymns in Revelation are often said to have a militant quality. They tell of the reign of God, the defeat of evil, and the salvation of God's people. This lecture gave examples of African American songs that draw themes from Revelation. In what way do these songs preserve the message of Revelation? In what way do these songs give the message of Revelation new and different qualities?

The Apocalypse and Social Progress
Lecture 21

C hristian communities often seem to take one of two paths in their approach to Revelation: Some Christian groups seem to be preoccupied with the book and what it might tell us about the future, and the rest don't read Revelation at all. In this lecture, we will briefly go back to colonial America, where interest in Revelation was common among Protestants. We will trace the "progressive" approach to Revelation, in which history was assumed to be progressing toward the millennial kingdom of God. People could share in this progressive march of history by spreading the gospel and reforming society. We will then look at the divergence of the apocalyptic and progressive perspectives, at which point some Christian groups dropped their interest in Revelation while retaining a hope for social progress and some hung on to Revelation but moved away from the hope for societal reform. We are still feeling the effects of that split today.

The Interpretation of Jonathan Edwards

- Jonathan Edwards was the leading American theologian of the mid-1700s and a man who was both deeply spiritual and deeply intellectual. He was involved in the religious awakenings that swept through New England during his time, and he produced extensive treatises on Scripture, theology, and the psychology of religion.

- Edwards had a theological view of history, and he sometimes summed it up in language from the Apocalypse that referred to God as the Alpha and the Omega, the beginning and the end. For Edwards, all things ultimately came from God and were moving back to God.

- Further, Edwards understood that all things were created good. He thought of Creation as the extension of God's goodness into space and history as the extension of God's goodness into time. Yet he recognized that both were marred by human sin.

- Edwards insisted that God had determined to work out his purposes providentially in order to restore all things to their proper state at the end of time. Revelation was helpful here, because its vision culminated in Creation itself being made new.

- Edwards read the Apocalypse as an outline of God's activity in history. Like some of the earlier interpreters we've seen, he thought the book outlined all of history, from the time of Christ to the end of the present age, and that each vision symbolized a particular era.

© The Teaching Company Collection.

- For Edwards, time had progressed up to the visions in Revelations 16, where angels pour out bowls of wrath on the beast and his

John Edwards was fascinated by the Apocalypse and kept notes on it throughout his life.

kingdom. Edwards thought that the pouring signified an outpouring of spiritual power on earth, bringing people to the true faith and overcoming the deceptive forces of the Antichrist, which Edwards believed was the papacy.

- Edwards also shared the older idea that history was moving toward the millennial age, envisioned as the final period of peace on earth before the dawn of the new Creation and the onset of eternity. At that time, knowledge and holiness would fill the earth; the divisions in the church would cease; and the entire human family would be united.

- For Edwards, this vision defined the goal of God's work in the world. Human beings could not achieve this ideal by their own efforts.

Edwards's Progressive Outlook

- As we've seen in previous lectures, it's unproductive to try to turn the Apocalypse into a timeline, but the progressive outlook of Edwards's approach has proved to be influential.

- Although Edwards insisted that God alone could create a truly peaceful and happy society, he assumed that people would want to direct their efforts toward that end. The idea that things were moving toward an ultimate goal gave people a strong sense of purpose and meant their work had value.

- For Edwards, the immediate focus was on the spiritual renewal of individuals and communities, but given that the millennium included the general expansion of knowledge, he could also celebrate and encourage advances that were being made in science. Such advances helped to raise the overall standard of living, bringing the millennial ideal closer.

Charles Finney and Post-Millennialism

- Edwards believed that God was the one who set the pace of history leading up to the millennium, but many in the 19th century thought that they could speed things up by working to reform society. Perhaps the best example of someone who wanted to get to the millennial age in a hurry was Charles Finney.

- Finney started out as a lawyer, but he had a conversion experience and became one of the most famous evangelists of the early 19th century. His brand of hard-hitting preaching was successful in getting thousands of people to commit themselves to the Christian faith. Finney also connected his evangelistic efforts to efforts at social reform, particularly in controlling alcohol abuse and abolishing slavery.

- All this combined attention to evangelism and social reform was part of a worldview called post-millennialism. The term refers to the idea that history will gradually progress toward the millennial age, and only after the millennium—or post-millennium—will Jesus return for the resurrection and last judgment.

William Lloyd Garrison

- In addition to Finney, other abolitionists had their own take on the apocalyptic visions of Revelation. Perhaps the best example of this group is the journalist William Lloyd Garrison, editor of a newspaper called *The Liberator*. Garrison sought no less than the complete and immediate abolition of slavery in America.

- For people like Garrison, Revelation's descriptions of the beast and Babylon didn't pertain to the papacy but to America, because its vast economic system relied on the practice of human slavery. The beast was active wherever people were in bondage.

- This perspective takes up aspects of the description of Babylon in Revelation 18. There, imperial Rome is depicted as a commercial power with a relentless appetite for goods, such as gold, jewels, cloth, and most disturbingly, "slaves and the souls of men."

- The abolitionists latched onto a phrase that was used in the same section of Revelation (18:4): "Come out of her my people, that ye not be partakers of her sins, and that ye receive not of her plagues." This served as a call to disengage from the economic practices associated with Babylon and gave the name to the most radical wing of the abolitionist movement: the Come-Outers.

The Outbreak of War

- The imagery of Revelation played a new role during the Civil War, calling people to take part in the struggle. One of the most influential uses of this imagery appeared in "The Battle Hymn of the Republic," written by Julia Ward Howe in 1861.

- The primary text on which the song is based is Revelation 19, which depicts the coming of the Lord to trample the great wine press of wrath. In that vision, the warrior is Christ, and the only weapon he uses is the sword that comes from his mouth. His terrible swift sword is his word, and it is truth that is the victor of the battle.

- The "Battle Hymn" uses very similar images to call people to commit themselves to what is good and just and true. Given the context in which it was written, some identify the song with military conflicts, but the imagery has also functioned in the suffragette and civil rights movements.

New Types of Biblical Interpretation

- After the Civil War was over, the apocalyptic and progressive impulses that had been linked for so long finally came apart. Apocalyptic rhetoric no longer seemed plausible. The country had been through a cataclysmic conflict, and while slavery was gone, the world still seemed far removed from the millennial ideal.

- The notion of the millennium itself lost much of its appeal. People in many of the mainline Protestant churches were moving away from the idea that Revelation offered an outline of history that would culminate in a 1,000-year period of peace.

- Those churches began to favor newer types of biblical interpretation that had developed in Europe. This newer perspective was to read the Bible historically and to ask what the texts meant in their original context. With the adoption of this approach, people began to see that Revelation was similar to other ancient apocalypses.

- At the same time, many people saw a sharp contrast between the Hebrew prophets and the apocalyptic writings. The prophets were valued because they seemed to call for greater efforts to achieve a just society in this world. But the apocalyptic writings fell out of favor because they were thought to be preoccupied with cosmic catastrophe and salvation in the age to come.

- Even as people let go of the apocalyptic dimension, many hung onto hope for the progressive improvement of society. In this sense, the legacy of the progressive view of God's work in history has been positive, encouraging people to work for renewal in the Christian community and for reforms within society.

Suggested Reading

McDermott, *One Holy and Happy Society*, chap. 2.

Moorhead, "Apocalypticism in Mainstream Protestantism."

Questions to Consider

1. Revelation supplied the idea that history would culminate in "the millennium," which many assumed would be a 1,000-year period of peace on earth. Religious leaders, such as Jonathan Edwards and Charles Finney, thought the millennium would come progressively and directed their efforts toward that end. What were some of the positive aspects of this approach? What were some of the problems with this approach?

2. In the decades after the Civil War, many Christians who were committed to the progressive reform of society distanced themselves from the apocalyptic perspectives of Revelation. What might they have gained by letting go of Revelation? What might they have lost by doing so?

Awaiting the End in 1844 and Beyond
Lecture 22

In this last lecture, we looked at a worldview known as post-millennialism, that is, the idea that the millennial age of peace and prosperity comes through progress. As we saw, post-millennialism lost its appeal after the Civil War, when society still seemed far short of reaching the golden age. Some people hung onto hope for progress in the church and in society, but they found it best to leave Revelation aside and to focus on texts that seemed more realistic. In this lecture, we will turn to the other side of the story and focus on those who decided that the movement of history was not positive but negative. Instead of dropping the apocalyptic dimension and maintaining the hope for progress, this pre-millennialist perspective hung onto the apocalyptic dimension and abandoned hope for progress. Those who held this perspective turned away from reforming society as a whole to focus on bringing individuals to faith and salvation.

The Adventist Perspective

- The word "advent" means "coming," and those who take the Adventist perspective have tried to determine the exact time that Christ's Second Coming will occur. As we have seen, efforts to make this determination have not been successful in the past. It is interesting to ask, however, why this line of thinking would appeal to some people.

- As we saw in the last lecture, those who hoped for continuing progress in history came to think of the future as something open; they envisioned a world of continual change that was moving into a future with no real sense of closure.

- The Adventists move in the opposite direction, seeking closure. They want to know that history has a goal that will be realized through a clear act of God. They want to affirm that God is in control, that God has a plan for the flow of history, and that the Bible reveals God's plans, so that we can determine where we are in the flow of events leading up to the end.

- What makes the Adventist impulse distinctive is that some who share it think the Bible not only reveals what God will do but when God will do it. This sets up situations of high expectation, followed by deep disappointment.

William Miller
- After narrowly escaping injury in the War of 1812, William Miller, originally a Deist, turned to Christianity and began attending a Baptist church.

- In his new faith, Miller read the Bible from beginning to end, with the goal of harmonizing all its apparent contradictions. During this process, he concluded that the Bible laid out God's plan for history and showed the time when Christ would return.

- Based on calculations derived from events in the book of Daniel, Miller estimated that the current period of history would end and the kingdom of God would come to earth in 1843 or 1844. His method of calculation represents a remarkable combination of literal and symbolic interpretation.

- In addition to images from the book of Daniel, Miller also used those from Revelation to symbolize periods of history. The seven-headed beast symbolized Rome under the papacy; the locusts that swarmed out of the abyss symbolized the rise of Islamic armies; and the horsemen who shot fire at their enemies were the armies of the Turks.

- In the 1840s, Miller's predictions attracted thousands of people and it became a widespread popular movement. Miller's followers even had their own newspaper, called *Signs of the Times*. Pressed for more clarity about when the end would come, Miller narrowed the time frame for Christ's return to sometime between March 21, 1843, and March 21, 1844.

- As the time approached, the movement grew in size, and followers became ever more aggressive in promoting the message. At the same time, opposition to the Millerites intensified. As the tension mounted, the Millerites came to believe that the images of the Antichrist symbolized not just the papacy but all the churches that opposed their message about the end.

Library of Congress.

Heirs of William Miller's movement include groups like the Seventh Day Adventists and Jehovah's Witnesses.

- When the time period Miller had identified passed with no sign of the end, pressure mounted to recalculate. One of Miller's followers made the audacious announcement that the true time of Christ's return would be October 22, 1844. The news spread rapidly throughout the movement.

- Critics of the movement lampooned the Millerites with cartoons depicting them sitting on hilltops or their roofs, wearing long white robes and looking up as they waited for Jesus. In reality, on the fateful day, most simply gathered in homes or churches and waited. When nothing happened, the day became known as the Great Disappointment.

Reactions to the Great Disappointment

- People seemed to have one of three main responses to the failure of Miller's prediction: rejection, reinterpretation, or recalculation.

- The first response, rejecting the idea that the Bible could be used to determine when the end would come, would seem to be the most obvious. Those who responded to the Great Disappointment in this way left the movement and tried to get on with their lives.

- The second response was to reinterpret what had happened. Some people concluded that Miller had been right about the date of Christ's coming but wrong about the mode of his coming. They insisted that Christ had come to cleanse the sanctuary at the time Miller predicted, but it was the heavenly sanctuary, not the earthly one.

- The idea that there is a sanctuary in heaven appears in the book of Hebrews and in Revelation 11:19. The verse in Revelation offers a vision of the heavenly temple being opened. Miller's followers drew on this and other New Testament texts to develop the idea that at the appointed time in 1844, Christ had entered the sanctuary in heaven. When his work there was done, he would come to earth.

- Those who responded to the Great Disappointment by reinterpreting Miller's predictions formed the nucleus of a group that would eventually become the Seventh Day Adventists. One of their early leaders was Ellen White, who experienced visions that included apocalyptic motifs and came to be regarded as a prophet by members of the Adventist circle.

- The third response to the Great Disappointment was to recalculate the time of Christ's coming yet again. Among those who persisted in these calculations was Charles Taze Russell. He began to publish a paper called *Zion's Watch Tower* to express his views, and along with it, he formed a group called Zion's Watch Tower Tract Society. Today, this group is known as the Jehovah's Witnesses.

Charles Taze Russell

- Russell was born a few years after the Great Disappointment, but he was intrigued with the idea of determining when the end would come. In his younger years, there was some speculation that the date might be 1874, but again, that year came and went without any cataclysmic change.

- Russell concluded that Christ must have returned spiritually in that year, which according to his new theory, marked the beginning of the period that he called the millennial dawn. It was a transitional period that he thought would end in 1914, with the establishment of the kingdom of God on earth.

- The beliefs of the Jehovah's Witnesses reflect a theological system that is created by combining various verses of the Bible. Russell connected a verse from Luke 21 with the plague scenes in Revelation 16 to picture a spiritual battle in which the false religious influences that dominated the churches were overthrown.

- A special feature of Russell's work was his interest in Revelation's vision of 144,000 people, who seemed to play a key role in the apocalyptic drama. In the original literary context, the number is simply a way of talking about the community of faith as a whole, but Russell thought it represented a specific number of people who would one day rule spiritually with Christ as priests and kings in heaven.

- When 1914 arrived and World War I broke out, it seemed like it might really be the year of the biblical Armageddon. But again, despite all the carnage on the battlefield, the new age failed to arrive. Russell's successor recalculated again and announced that the resurrection of the dead would occur in 1925. When that failed to occur, many left the movement and others became more circumspect about how close the end might be.

- The Adventist impulse was to seek closure, but closure is precisely what proved to be so elusive. The groups that emerged after the Great Disappointment may have reinterpreted what happened or tried to recalculate the time of the end, but finally, they could survive only by living with a sense of ambiguity. They had to return to the idea that there would be an end someday, but just when it would come remains an open question.

Suggested Reading

O'Leary, *Arguing the Apocalypse*.

Penton, "The Eschatology of the Jehovah's Witnesses."

Questions to Consider

1. The movements in this lecture have focused attention on the imminent ending of the present age. What factors might initially attract people to this message?

2. When the predictions that the current age will end at a specific time have proven wrong, several responses are possible. Why might some simply leave the movement? Why might others try to reinterpret the predictions to fit experience? Why might others consider setting another date for the end?

Rapture, Tribulation, and Armageddon
Lecture 23

W e now come to the perspective that seems to dominate modern popular perceptions of Revelation: the scenario that begins when all faithful Christians are whisked up from the earth into heaven in the event known as the Rapture. Afterwards, the rest of humanity will be left behind to face the terrors that occur during the reign of the Antichrist. This scenario blends various parts of the Bible together with some of the places we hear about in the daily news, and in its depictions of a campaign of terror culminating in Armageddon, it contributes to the idea that Revelation is a book to be feared. In this lecture, we will look at this Dispensationalist system in more detail and ask why it has become so popular. We will also note the problems it creates and explore how it relates to alternatives that seem more promising.

Dispensationalism

- Dispensationalism is a form of pre-millennialism, the belief system that expects the world to get progressively worse until the return of Christ. Unlike the Adventists, the Dispensationalists refuse to set a specific date for Christ's arrival; they say that the end could come at any time.

- This belief system is called Dispensationalism because it divides history into blocks of time called "dispensations." The dispensations began with the Creation and are to end with New Jerusalem.

- Those who follow this approach believe that prophecy is history written in advance. The prophetic passages in the Bible constitute a script that must be played out at the end of the age, although no single book of the Bible contains the entire script.

- Dispensationalism originated with John Nelson Darby, who lived in Britain in the early 1800s. His views became widely known through a series of Bible conferences held in the United States.

132

- In the late 1800s, the evangelist Dwight L. Moody picked up Darby's approach. His preaching conveyed an ominous sense of a world in decline, which gave greater urgency to his appeal that people should come to faith before it's too late.

- In the 1970s, Hal Lindsey put this approach into his book *The Late Great Planet Earth*. Lindsey wove passages from the Bible together with news headlines from the *Washington Post* and *New York Times*. Many found his picture of a world heading rapidly toward Armageddon believable.

Dwight L. Moody's large evangelistic rallies were very successful.

- Tim LaHaye and Jerry Jenkins incorporated the system into a series of novels called *Left Behind*. These novels wove Dispensationalism into a fictional plot about people who missed out on the Rapture and had to survive on earth during the time of the Antichrist.

A Combined Futuristic Scenario

- Dispensationalism is not simply a reading of Revelation but a theological system that combines various parts of the Bible into a distinctive futuristic picture.

- A basic feature of the system is that it makes a sharp distinction between the history of the Jewish people and the history of the church. Dispensationalists disagree that Christians share in the promises made to the people of Israel in the Old Testament. They insist that the Old Testament prophecies concerning Israel must be literally fulfilled in the national history of the Jewish people.

- According to the book of Genesis, God promised that Abraham's descendants would possess the land that extends from the River Euphrates to the River of Egypt. Given that this promise has not literally been fulfilled in the past, Dispensationalists argue that it must be fulfilled in the future, at the end of the age.

- They further argue that the reason for God's delay in fulfilling the promise is that in the 1st century, the Jewish people rejected Jesus as their Messiah. Thus, God postponed his promise of the land, and a church comprised largely of Gentiles came into existence.

- Dispensationalists are waiting for this Gentile church to be miraculously removed from the earth at the Rapture. That will be the signal that time is moving forward again, and when that occurs, Christ will come to establish his kingdom on earth, with Jerusalem as its capital. That will complete God's purposes for the Jewish people and mark the turn of the ages.

- A key text for this system of thought is Daniel 9, which outlines the period extending from the restoration of Jerusalem in the 5th century B.C. until the end of the age. Daniel says that the period will consist of 70 blocks of time, each lasting for 7 years. But God stopped the progression of this prophetic history when Jesus came and most Jewish people rejected him.

- The Dispensationalists assume that when God restarts the clock of prophecy, the church will be mysteriously taken up from earth to heaven in the Rapture. This idea is taken from the passage in Paul's First Letter to the Thessalonians, where the followers of Jesus are caught up to meet the Lord in the air.

- The belief that Dispensationalists will escape the tribulations that occur in the middle of Revelation is reinforced by the fact that the word "church" is used elsewhere in the book but not in the middle.

- For Dispensationalists, the visions of Revelation are to be taken as literally as possible, although it's important to note that this view is selectively literal. Further, the Dispensationalist approach tends to ignore the visions of hope that are interspersed with the scenes of disaster in Revelation.

- The Dispensational scenario draws heavily on the picture of the Antichrist that was developed in the ancient church, essentially a composite image of a tyrant drawn from Revelation, First and Second John, and Second Thessalonians.

Modern Interpretations of Ancient Biblical Scenes

- The Dispensationalist perspective assumes that modern readers are better equipped than ancient ones to understand the predictions of the Bible because we are closer to the final events.

- For example, one futuristic scenario weaves in a battle scene from the book of Ezekiel, where a mysterious figure called Gog attacks Israel from the north. Popular forms of Dispensationalism usually identify Gog with Russia, which may seem reasonable to modern Western readers but would probably not have occurred to people in antiquity.

- Dispensationalists also assume that the present age will end with the battle of Armageddon, which is, of course, a name that comes from Revelation. But the system extends the name to a sequence of battles that combine scenes from Isaiah, Joel, Zechariah, and Revelation.

- In the popular imagination, Armageddon usually involves high-tech military weaponry. Recall, however, that in Revelation, only one weapon is mentioned: the sword from the mouth of Christ that symbolizes his word.

The Appeal of Dispensationalism

- The phenomenon of Dispensationalism is appealing in part because it gives people a strong sense of divine control over history. The Bible predicted that the world would get worse, so it's no surprise that we are faced with war, poverty, and the degradation of the environment. Yet despite appearances of chaos, God has a plan.

- Of course, some people might be horrified at the idea that God would create this kind of a violent script for the future of the world, but in the Dispensationalist view, it is better to think of a God who is in control than to think of a world that is totally out of control.

- Note, too, that the system makes a place for human freedom. It assumes that the course of history has been set by God, and no one can change the direction the world is going. But people can change the direction of their lives by coming to faith; when they do so, they can be assured of experiencing the Rapture.

- The theme of the Rapture plays a central role in the hope for personal salvation. It gives people the promise of escape from suffering. When the book of Revelation was first written, it called people to persevere in the face of challenges, but the Rapture idea changes the emphasis from perseverance to escape.

- A final reason for the appeal of Dispensationalism is that it gives people a way to make sense of experiences in the modern world. Hal Lindsey's book *The Late Great Planet Earth* was a notable example of this. Lindsey emphasized that the establishment of the modern state of Israel was a sign that the millennial age was drawing near. Yet the system of Dispensationalism remains adaptable because its proponents always stop short of setting a specific date for the end.

- Throughout this course, we have explored Revelation in ways that are quite different from the Dispensational approach, and we've seen that the book itself subverts any attempts to turn it into a map of history. We've also seen that examining Revelation in its own historical context does not make the book less relevant for modern readers. In fact, by asking how the book was relevant at the time it was written, we can see how it remains relevant for us today.

Suggested Reading

Boyer, *When Time Shall Be No More*.

Sandeen, *The Roots of Fundamentalism*.

Questions to Consider

1. The lecture noted that the Dispensationalist method of weaving Revelation into a scenario of the future appeals to people for various reasons. One is that it affirms that current events seem chaotic, but God is ultimately in control. The other is that it offers people hope that by coming to faith now, they will escape the worst when it comes. Do these observations seem convincing to you? If so, why? If not, why not?

2. Popular forms of the Dispensationalist approach sometimes suggest direct connections between passages from Revelation and current events. Why might some people be drawn to this use of the Bible? Why might others be critical of this use of the Bible?

The Modern Apocalyptic Renaissance
Lecture 24

Throughout this course, we've considered the incredible impact the Apocalypse has had on people over the centuries since it was written. Our purpose in showing the range of possible interpretations of Revelation from ancient times until now has been to underscore the importance of reading it constructively, to allow it to open up ways of seeing that challenge and benefit us as readers. In this final lecture, we will explore modern scholarship on the Apocalypse, which has shown that the book engages the world in a fashion that is both critical and constructive.

Ernst Käsemann and the Renewal of Apocalypticism

- As noted in an earlier lecture, some scholars in the 19th century began to shift their studies away from apocalyptic writings to the writings of the Hebrew prophets. In the 20th century and more recently, however, there has been a renaissance of interest in apocalyptic writings that has opened up some rewarding perspectives.

- In 1960, a German New Testament scholar named Ernst Käsemann declared that "apocalyptic was the mother of all Christian theology." He made that comment in an essay that pointed to the early church's conviction that the death and resurrection of Jesus disclosed God's commitment to set things right in the world. It was a perspective in which hope for the future intruded into the present.

- For Käsemann, the question at the heart of apocalypticism was the following: Who was really Lord over the world? Käsemann focused on this question because he saw competition among various powers in the world for people's loyalties. Specifically, Nazism as an ideology, along with Hitler's rise to power, had created a situation of competing truth claims.

- On one side were the claims of the state. Nazism operated with a racist ideology in which people of Aryan descent were declared to be inherently superior to all others. Further, the Nazis developed a kind of cult around Hitler's leadership.

- On the other side of the conflict was the Confessing Church, a group that resisted the attempts of the Nazis to impose their racist ideology on the Protestants in Germany.

- The devastating consequences of Nazi ideology showed Käsemann that fundamental commitments mattered. For Käsemann, the results of Hitler's attempt to rule the earth—death camps and ruined cities—were the opposite of the lordship of God and his Messiah. Käsemann knew that God's purposes were ultimately redemptive, and this is where the apocalyptic tradition was so important.

- Käsemann had been disturbed by people who seemed to privatize their faith, to set it aside from the rest of life. The apocalyptic tradition did not allow people to compartmentalize things, as if heaven mattered and earth did not.

- In writing about Revelation, Käsemann asked the question: To whom does the world belong? The idea here is that basic commitments matter. In every generation, people base their lives on the beliefs and values they hold most deeply, and these shape the way they see the present and the future. Revelation presses people to keep the horizon broad enough to include God's determination to make all things new.

- Revelation was composed by a writer who saw a clash between the claims of the empire—the beast—and the claims of his faith—the Lamb. The beast wins victory by subjugating others, while the Lamb wins victory through the power of his self-sacrifice. Where the beast seeks dominion by wielding the power of death, the Lamb's victory leads through death toward the ultimate gift of life.

- This way of reading Revelation does not treat the vision of the beast as a prediction of a distant figure known as the Antichrist. Rather, it recognizes that the imagery was designed to startle readers into seeing the destructive side of the dominant political ideology.

- Revelation points to a future that is ultimately beyond the capacity of any human being to create, yet keeping that vision in mind can also shape perspectives on the present. It does so by calling people to resist the forces that diminish life, while encouraging a sense of hope and renewed commitment to the world God has made and will make new.

Revelation's Link to the Prophetic Tradition
- This interplay between challenging people in the present, while calling them to hope for the future, has encouraged some scholars to revisit the question of Revelation's link to the prophetic tradition.

- As we've said, for many years, there was a tendency among scholars to separate the prophetic writings, which focused on ethical issues and urged people to engage with the present world, and the apocalyptic writings, which were seen as speculative and otherworldly. As scholars gave renewed attention to apocalyptic literature, however, they began to see that all these texts fall along a spectrum.

- The prophetic writings certainly include hope for a more just society on earth, but they went outside the realm of ordinary existence when they envisioned an end to death and the onset of a new heaven and a new earth. When the prophetic texts expanded the horizon of hope to that point, they were not far from what the apocalyptic writers were saying.

- The discovery of the Dead Sea Scrolls right after World War II helped scholars see that ancient Judaism was much more diverse than had been previously thought. Some scrolls, such as the War Scroll, included both apocalyptic and non-apocalyptic elements.

- The complexity continued as scholars turned to the world of early Christianity. Everyone knew that Revelation was an apocalypse, yet its opening lines also claimed that it was a book of prophecy, and it drew heavily on the language and imagery of the Hebrew prophets. In turn, seeing Revelation as part of the broader prophetic tradition has encouraged people to see that its visions pertain to both the present and future.

The Globalization of Biblical Studies

- The academic study of the Bible was traditionally centered in Europe and North America, but voices from around the globe have now joined in the discussion and added to the sense of urgency surrounding Revelation's message.

- Some of the voices in the global discussion have come from Latin America, where many have had to struggle with issues of political oppression and poverty. In the context of these problems, some have found that Revelation's imagery offers a way to name the powers of violence and oppression while giving people a reason to persevere.

- Elisabeth Schüssler Fiorenza was one scholar who had a keen sense that Revelation's vision of God's work in the world extended to all facets of life. Her book, *Revelation: Vision of a Just World*, showed how Revelation challenged the social and political forces that diminished human life and called for people to engage in the struggle against them.

- In North America, the circle of discussion now includes African American voices, who have added new dimensions to the interpretation of Revelation. An African American scholar named Brian Blount, for example, has identified the central theme of witness in Revelation, meaning telling the truth in situations where the truth is disputed.

- The African American tradition that we discussed earlier in the course has helped us see that the Apocalypse can be remarkably candid about the dispiriting side of life, yet it also battles against the forces that bring despair by drawing people toward a future that is not defined by the present moment.

Revelation's Power to Challenge and Encourage

- Revelation has an unparalleled ability to both challenge and encourage its readers, and both aspects work together to create its powerful effect. Where the author sees evil at work, his writing is hard-hitting and confrontational, but when he speaks of hope, he gives us radiance. The key to understanding the book is to move through the challenging scenes into these visions of hope.

- Hope is built into the very structure of Revelation. The writer is not content to hold back the promise until the end. He gives it to readers repeatedly as he tells the story of God's victory over the forces that destroy life and drive people to despair. Each great cycle of visions in the Apocalypse moves through scenes that disturb readers back to the presence of God and the Lamb.

- It's also true that for every transition from threat to promise, Revelation gives us a song, to which other musicians have added their voices. When you think of the Apocalypse, think of the Hallelujah Chorus or of the saints marching in, because that is the direction that the book pulls its readers: toward the goal of hope and life.

Suggested Reading

Rhoads, *From Every People and Nation.*

Schüssler Fiorenza, *Revelation.*

1. Can you identify one aspect of the book of Revelation or its affect on Western culture that you found especially engaging? What makes this insight significant for you?

2. Revelation is a book that has traditionally been read within the Christian community. Does the book offer helpful food for thought to those who are not connected to the Christian community? If so, what might those insights be?

Bibliography

Allison, Dale C., Jr. *Constructing Jesus: Memory, Imagination, and History*. Grand Rapids, MI: Baker Academic, 2010. A major study of the historical Jesus that gives extended treatment to the question of Jesus's relationship to the apocalyptic tradition.

———. "The Eschatology of Jesus." In *The Encyclopedia of Apocalypticism*. Vol. 1, *The Origins of Apocalypticism in Judaism and Christianity*, edited by John J. Collins, 267–302. New York: Continuum, 1998. A clear summary of the main scholarly viewpoints concerning Jesus's views about the future, along with a balanced treatment of the main New Testament passages in the debate.

Aune, David E. "The Influence of Roman Court Ceremonial on the Apocalypse of John." In *Apocalypticism, Prophecy, and Magic in Early Christianity: Collected Essays*, 99–119. Grand Rapids: Baker Academic, 2006. A study of the way Revelation's description of God's heavenly throne hall uses images of Roman court ceremonies to counter the claims of the empire.

Barr, David L. "Doing Violence: Moral Issues in Reading John's Apocalypse." In *Reading the Book of Revelation: A Resource for Students*, 97–108. Atlanta: Society of Biblical Literature, 2003. A reflective analysis of ways in which scholars have understood Revelation's violent scenes and how the imagery can be understood in light of Christ as the Lamb.

Bauckham, Richard. *The Climax of Prophecy: Studies on the Book of Revelation*. Edinburgh: T. & T. Clark, 1993. A collection of essays on major aspects of Revelation, including its use of traditions concerning Nero, its economic critique of the empire, and its expansive visions of hope for the nations.

———. *The Theology of the Book of Revelation*. Cambridge: Cambridge University Press, 1993. This overview of theological themes gives special attention to Revelation's understanding of God, Jesus, the Spirit of prophecy, and the nature of hope for the future.

Blount, Brian K. *Can I Get a Witness? Reading Revelation through African American Culture*. Louisville, KY: Westminster John Knox, 2005. Written from an African American perspective, this book enhances our understanding of Revelation's call for active resistance in the face of injustice and the militant quality of music in community life.

Boring, M. Eugene. *Revelation*. Louisville, KY: John Knox Press, 1989. A readable discussion of Revelation that offers helpful comments on each chapter of the book.

Boyer, Paul. *When Time Shall Be No More: Prophecy Belief in Modern American Culture*. Cambridge, MA, and London: Belknap Press of Harvard University, 1992. A valuable study of the modern American religious groups that seem to thrive on the belief that the world is nearing its end.

Collins, Adela Yarbro. *Crisis and Catharsis: The Power of the Apocalypse*. Philadelphia: Westminster John Knox, 1984. A study of the origins of Revelation that argues that the book was not so much a response to a clear crisis of persecution as it was a work designed to provoke its readers into seeing problems that were not readily apparent.

Collins, John J. *The Apocalyptic Imagination: An Introduction to Jewish Apocalyptic Literature*. 2nd ed. Grand Rapids, MI: Eerdmans, 1998. This is one of the best introductions to the field of Jewish apocalyptic writing, with helpful comments on most of the major texts from the 2nd century B.C. to the 2nd century A.D.

Daley, Brian E. "Apocalypticism in Early Christian Theology." In *The Encyclopedia of Apocalypticism*. Vol. 2, *Apocalypticism in Western History and Culture*, edited by Bernard McGinn, 3–47. New York: Continuum, 1998. A survey of apocalyptic themes in Christian sources from the 2nd to the 6th centuries A.D., with attention to the changing social contexts in which these texts were written.

de Boer, Martin C. "Paul and Apocalyptic Eschatology." In *The Encyclopedia of Apocalypticism*. Vol. 1, *The Origins of Apocalypticism in Judaism and Christianity*, edited by John J. Collins, 345–83. New York: Continuum, 1998. A helpful introduction to the role of apocalyptic thinking in the letters of Paul.

deSilva, David A. "2 Esdras: The Mighty One Has Not Forgotten." In *Introducing the Apocrypha: Message, Context, and Significance*, 323–51. Grand Rapids, MI: Baker Academic, 2002. A good introduction to one of the classic Jewish apocalypses that is printed in many editions of the Bible but is not formally considered to be part of the biblical canon.

————. *Seeing Things John's Way: The Rhetoric of the Book of Revelation.* Louisville, KY: Westminster John Knox, 2009. A study of the way that the language and form of Revelation help to shape readers' perspectives on God, the world, and their own situations.

Fredriksen, Paula. "Tyconius and Augustine on the Apocalypse." In *The Apocalypse in the Middle Ages*, edited by Richard K. Emmerson and Bernard McGinn, 20–37. Ithaca, NY, and London: Cornell University Press, 1992. An introduction to the pivotal role that Tyconius and Augustine played in developing a spiritual interpretation of the Apocalypse that became dominant in the ancient and medieval church.

Friesen, Steven J. "The Beast from the Land: Revelation 13:11–18 and Social Setting." In *Reading the Book of Revelation: A Resource for Students*, edited by David L. Barr, 49–64. Atlanta: Society of Biblical Literature, 2003. Using insights from archaeology, this essay considers the way Revelation critiques the role of elite urban families in promoting the imperial cult in Asia Minor.

————. *Imperial Cults and the Apocalypse of John: Reading Revelation in the Ruins.* Oxford and New York: Oxford University Press, 2001. A fascinating study of the cult of the Roman emperors in Asia Minor, including its archaeological remains and the implications of this material for interpreting Revelation.

Heschel, Abraham. *The Prophets: An Introduction*. New York: Harper & Row, 1962. A classic study that gives readers a vivid sense of the character of the Hebrew prophets and the key dimensions of their message.

Hill, Charles E. *Regnum Caelorum: Patterns of Millennial Thought in Early Christianity*. 2nd ed. Grand Rapids, MI: Eerdmans, 2001. This is a helpful survey of the way Christian writers from the 2nd and 3rd centuries looked at the future, especially the question of whether there would be a 1,000-year messianic kingdom on earth.

Koester, Craig R. *Revelation and the End of All Things*. Grand Rapids, MI: Eerdmans, 2001. Written for a broad readership, this book sketches out the history of interpretation of Revelation and provides comments on each chapter of the book.

————. "Roman Slave Trade and the Critique of Babylon in Revelation 18." *Catholic Biblical Quarterly* 70 (2008): 766–86. A study of the archeological evidence for the slave trade in Asia Minor and the critique of this practice found in the imagery of Revelation.

Kraybill, J. N. *Imperial Cult and Commerce in John's Apocalypse*. Sheffield: Sheffield Academic Press, 1996. An overview of Roman commercial and religious practices and the implications for understanding Revelation's critique of the empire.

Krey, Philip D. W. "Luther and the Apocalypse: Between Christ and History." In *Biblical and Theological Perspectives on Eschatology*, edited by Carl E. Braaten and Robert W. Jenson, 135–45. Grand Rapids, MI: Eerdmans, 2002. A brief overview of Luther's evolving interpretations of the book of Revelation.

Mabee, Carleton. *Sojourner Truth: Slave, Prophet, Legend*. New York and London: New York University Press, 1993. A biography of a leading African American reformer from the 19th century.

McDermott, Gerald R. "That Glorious Work of God and the Beautiful Society: The Premillennial Age and the Millennium." In *One Holy and Happy Society: The Public Theology of Jonathan Edwards*, chapter 2. University Park, PA: Pennsylvania State University Press, 1992. A study of the hope of Jonathan Edwards that the kingdom of God would progressively be established on earth.

McDonald, Lee Martin. *The Formation of the Christian Biblical Canon*. Rev. ed. Peabody, MA: Hendrickson, 1995. A balanced assessment of the way in which early Christians identified books that would be included among their authoritative Scriptures.

McGinn, Bernard. *Antichrist: Two Thousand Years of the Human Fascination with Evil*. New York: Columbia University Press, 2000. A fascinating study of traditions concerning the Antichrist, from the Jewish antecedents to the early Christian synthesis, and the changing interpretations throughout Christian history.

————. *Apocalyptic Spirituality: Treatises and Letters of Lactantius, Adso of Montier en-Der, Joachim of Fiore, the Franciscan Spirituals, Savonarola*. Classics of Western Spirituality. Mahwah, NJ: Paulist Press, 1979. A collection of translations of apocalyptic texts that were composed between the 3rd and 15th centuries.

————. "Apocalypticism and Church Reform: 1100–1500." In *The Encyclopedia of Apocalypticism*. Vol. 2, *Apocalypticism in Western History and Culture*, edited by Bernard McGinn, 74–109. New York: Continuum, 1998. A helpful survey of the major apocalyptic perspectives of the late Middle Ages and their relationship to tensions among the empire, the papacy, and reform movements within the church.

Moorhead, James H. "Apocalypticism in Mainstream Protestantism, 1800 to the Present." In *The Encyclopedia of Apocalypticism*. Vol. 3, *Apocalypticism in the Modern Period and the Contemporary Age*, edited by Stephen J. Stein, 72–107. New York: Continuum, 1998. An overview of the way in which the Protestant hope for the progressive coming of God's kingdom gave way to a more open-ended sense of the future that no longer had an apocalyptic vision.

Murphy, Frederick J. *Fallen Is Babylon: The Revelation to John*. Harrisburg, PA: Trinity Press International, 1998. A sustained discussion of Revelation that offers insights on each chapter from a historical perspective.

Murrin, Michael. "Newton's Apocalypse." In *Newton and Religion: Context, Nature, and Influence*, edited by James E. Force, 203–20. Dordrecht, Boston, and London: Kluwer Academic Publishers, 1999. A good introduction to Isaac Newton's interpretation of Revelation, which sets his approach in the context of his time.

Nickelsburg, George W. E. *Jewish Literature between the Bible and the Mishnah*. 2nd ed. Minneapolis: Fortress Press, 2005. A useful introduction to the wide range of Jewish texts that were written between the 4th century B.C. and the 2nd century A.D.

O'Leary, Stephen D. *Arguing the Apocalypse: A Theory of Millennial Rhetoric*. New York: Oxford University Press, 1994. This book offers insights into the reasons that some people in 19th- and 20th-century America have been attracted to the belief that the end of the world is at hand.

Penton, M. J. "The Eschatology of the Jehovah's Witnesses: A Short Critical Analysis." In *The Coming Kingdom: Essays in American Millennialism and Eschatology*, edited by M. Darrol Bryant and Donald W. Dayton, 169–207. Barrytown, NY: New Era Books, 1983. An introduction to the beliefs of the Jehovah's Witnesses about the future and how these beliefs have changed over time.

Petersen, Rodney L. *Preaching in the Last Days: The Theme of the 'Two Witnesses' in the 16th and 17th Centuries*. New York: Oxford University Press, 1993. This study of the two witnesses from chapter 11 of Revelation offers insights into the way Revelation was understood during the Protestant Reformation.

Potestà, Gian Luca. "Radical Apocalyptic Movements in the Late Middle Ages." In *The Encyclopedia of Apocalypticism*. Vol. 2, *Apocalypticism in Western History and Culture*, edited by Bernard McGinn, 110–42. New York: Continuum, 1998. A helpful overview of the way apocalyptic thinking shaped medieval reform movements, such as the Spiritual Franciscans, the Fraticelli, and the Lollards.

Reeves, Marjorie. *Joachim of Fiore and the Prophetic Future: A Medieval Study in Historical Thinking*. Stroud: Sutton Publishing, 1999. An introduction to the thought of Joachim of Fiore and an account of his impact on Catholic and Protestant perspectives.

Rhoads, David, ed. *From Every People and Nation: The Book of Revelation in Intercultural Perspective*. Minneapolis: Fortress Press, 2005. A collection of essays showing the breadth of new perspectives on Revelation, including contributions by Latin American, African American, and Asian authors.

Rossing, Barbara R. *The Choice between Two Cities: Whore, Bride, and Empire in the Apocalypse*. Harrisburg, PA: Trinity Press International, 1999. A study of the way Revelation adapts and transforms contrasting feminine images in order to shape the readers' manner of life in the imperial world.

Sandeen, Ernest. *The Roots of Fundamentalism: British and American Millenarianism, 1800–1930*. Chicago: University of Chicago Press, 1970. This book explores the origins and early history of the futuristic perspectives that have been common among conservative evangelical Protestants.

Schüssler Fiorenza, Elisabeth. "Apokalypsis and Propheteia: Revelation in the Context of Early Christian Prophecy." In *The Book of Revelation: Justice and Judgment*. Philadelphia: Fortress Press, 1985. An examination of the relationship of early Christian prophecy to the tradition of Hebrew prophecy and the role that prophets played in ancient Christian communities.

———. *Revelation: Vision of a Just World*. Minneapolis: Fortress Press, 1991. An introduction to Revelation that focuses on the central theme of justice and is informed by feminist interpretations of the Bible and liberation theology.

Stapert, Calvin R. *Handel's Messiah: Comfort for God's People.* Grand Rapids, MI: Eerdmans, 2010. A highly readable study of the origins and message of Handel's *Messiah*, as well as interpretive notes on each part of the piece.

Stylianopoulios, Theodore. "'I Know Your Works': Grace and Judgment in the Apocalypse." In *Apocalyptic Thought in Early Christianity*, edited by Robert J. Daly, 17–32. Grand Rapids, MI: Baker Academic, 2009. Discusses theological tensions surrounding accountability for one's works and promises of mercy in Revelation's approach to final judgment.

Thompson, Leonard L. *The Book of Revelation: Apocalypse and Empire.* New York and Oxford: Oxford University Press, 1990. Argues that most Christians in the time of Domitian were relatively well adjusted to imperial rule, so that the Apocalypse presented a perspective that differed from that of many of its intended readers.

Tyson, John R. *Assist Me to Proclaim: The Life and Hymns of Charles Wesley.* Grand Rapids, MI: Eerdmans, 2008. An accessible study of the musical contributions of Charles Wesley and the times in which he lived and worked.

Vanderkam, James C. *The Dead Sea Scrolls Today.* 2nd ed. Grand Rapids, MI: Eerdmans, 2010. One of the best introductions to the Dead Sea Scrolls, including sections on the origins of the scrolls, the viewpoints in these texts, and scholarly debates about their significance.

van Henten, Jan Willem. "Dragon Myth and Imperial Ideology in Revelation 12–13." In *The Reality of Apocalypse: Rhetoric and Politics in the Book of Revelation*, edited by David L. Barr, 181–203. Atlanta: Society of Biblical Literature, 2006. An exploration of the use of images from Greco-Roman myths to support Roman imperialism and Revelation's use of mythic imagery to counter those claims.

Wainwright, Arthur W. *Mysterious Apocalypse: Interpreting the Book of Revelation.* Nashville, TN: Abingdon Press, 1993. A survey of the history of interpretation of Revelation from ancient times to the present.

Music Credits

Cantata No. 140, "Wachet auf, ruft uns die Stimme," BWV 140 courtesy of Haenssler Classic.

Music supplied by Getty Images.

When The Saints Go Marching In by Yanis S. Sousa—Premiumbeat.com.